Remembering
the Christian Past

ROBERT L. WILKEN

WILLIAM B. EERDMANS PUBLISHING COMPANY
GRAND RAPIDS, MICHIGAN

Printed in the United States of America

00 99 98 97 96 95   7 6 5 4 3 2 1

ISBN 0-8028-0880-8

The author and publisher gratefully acknowledge permission to reprint previously published material granted by the institutions listed in the source note to each chapter.

Contents

Introduction

A GENERATION AGO it was customary in Lutheran circles for pastors to devote two years to teaching young people Luther's Small Catechism. I once heard of a pastor in St. Louis, Missouri, whose practice it was to divide the two years of instruction as follows: "The first year," he said, "I have the students memorize the Catechism. The second year I tell them what it means."

I first learned of this pastor when I was a young man, and like others my age I guffawed. How ridiculous! The whole point of catechism instruction is to help young people understand the meaning of the Lord's Prayer, the Ten Commandments, the Creed. What is the value of having youngsters memorize the words of the Catechism without telling them what they mean? Now years later I realize that this pastor was much wiser than I. He knew that Christian faith was a matter of words, and that what counted most in the Catechism were the words. To be sure, the words signified things and carried meanings, but religious meaning is not univocal. As we mature it grows and deepens, bending and turning as our lives bend and turn.

Meaning is ephemeral, and the meanings one learns at twelve years of age are not the fullness of the words one memorizes. If a young person is fitted out only with the meanings of youth, what does one return to when the words are faded and forgotten? Words, however, endure, and if one has the words the meaning is never wholly lost. Words also have power to stir the heart, as Augustine knew well. "In my needy life, Lord, my heart is much exercised under the impact made by the *words* of your Holy Scripture" (*Conf.* 12.1.1).

I thought of this pastor as I sat down to write an introduction to the essays collected in this volume. I belong to a generation of Christian thinkers for whom meaning has been sovereign. The chief task of the Christian intellectual, it was thought, was to translate the words of the Bible and the theological tradition into the "meaningful" language and concepts of our day. Translation is, of course, an essential intellectual task, whether it be rendering a text from one language to another or translating words and ideas from one cultural idiom to another. But what if one can no longer recite the Ten Commandments or the Creed or has forgotten what one is translating?

The essays in this volume are a modest effort in remembering aspects of Christian tradition that have been forgotten. All touch on issues that are currently under discussion but in thinkers who lived long ago and in cultural settings distant from our own. Yet they address, if not directly, questions of our day — for example, religious pluralism, Christian apologetics, the biblical roots of the doctrine of the Trinity, the spiritual interpretation of the Bible, examples in the formation of a virtuous life, the place of the passions in our relation to God. The first essay, "Who Will Speak *for* the Religious Tradition?", was my presidential address at the American Academy of Religion in 1989 and is concerned with the role of commitment in the study of religion. The final essay discusses Christian thinking as a form of apprenticeship. All knowing begins with what we have received; before we become masters we must learn to be disciples, to allow others to form our words and guide our thoughts. In this spirit these essays were written and in this spirit they are gathered in this volume, thanks to the interest and encouragement of William B. Eerdmans, Jr.

ROBERT L. WILKEN

I

Who Will Speak *for* the Religious Traditions?

T HE FIRST YEAR I began studying Greek I recall the instructor passed out a diagram illustrating the meanings of the many Greek prepositions. At the center of the sheet was a circle and the prepositions were located at different points in relation to the circle. One preposition was *in* the circle, another *outside* the circle, one sat on a line *through* the circle, others were *alongside* it, *above* it, or *below* it. Prepositions, we learned, signified relations between things, persons, and ideas, and without a clear grasp of how the prepositions worked it was impossible to understand Greek or any language.

Prepositions are the joints and hinges that hold together conceptions about scholarship and teaching in the field of religion, as can be seen in the expressions we use to depict our common intellectual endeavor. I am referring of course to the phrases: the study *of* religion and teaching *about* religion. These expressions have become so commonplace that it is easy to forget

Presidential address to the American Academy of Religion, 22 November 1989, Anaheim, CA, published in *Journal of the American Academy of Religion 57*, no. 4 (1989): 699-717. Reprinted with permission.

that they have a history and have achieved canonical status only in recent times. Underneath them lie notions about religion that are relative newcomers to our intellectual life. Western thinkers, writes Jonathan Z. Smith, have only "had the last few centuries in which to imagine religion." In this view, religion "is solely the creation of the scholar's study. It is created for the scholar's analytic purposes by . . . imaginative acts of comparison and generalization. Religion has no independent existence apart from the academy. For this reason, the study of religion, and most particularly the historian of religion, must be relentlessly self-conscious. . . . For the self-conscious student of religion, no datum possesses intrinsic interest. It is of value only insofar as it can serve as *exempli gratia* of some fundamental issue in the imagination of religion."[1]

Viewed in this light the phrases "study of religion" and "teaching about religion" signify more than the adoption of a new vocabulary to designate a traditional area of inquiry.[2] The prepositions "of" and "about" portend a profound redefinition of the subject matter that requires, in turn, a new relation between the scholar and the thing studied. Consider, for example, some common expressions. In speaking of the teaching and study of literature or history in the colleges and universities, we say "she is studying Chaucer" or "teaching the American Revolution" or "he is an English teacher." Likewise in speaking of religious topics, it is customary to say that someone "studies the Quran" or "teaches the Bhagavadgita." However, if we say someone is a "religion teacher" or "teaches religion" the expressions carry unwelcome

1. Jonathan Z. Smith, *Imagining Religion: From Babylon to Jonestown* (Chicago, 1982), xi.

2. For a brief history of the shift perspective see Harold E. Remus, F. Stanley Lusby, and Linda M. Tober, "Religion as an Academic Discipline," in *Encyclopedia of the American Religious Experience* (1988), 3:1653-1669, and J. Samuel Preus, *Explaining Religion: Criticism and Theory from Bodin to Freud* (New Haven, 1987).

overtones, at least for the scholarly community. I am sure that some of you have had the experience at one of these meetings of stepping into a taxi with a chatty cabdriver. When the cabdriver heard what we do, he said: "So you are religion teachers?" There was an embarrassed silence and in chorus the group answered, "Oh, no, we are teachers *of* religion."

In ordinary speech the terms "teach" and "study" imply another term, "learn." What one means by "learning" will of course vary depending on the subject matter. To learn calculus requires that the student understand a system of thought as well as master certain skills, whereas for the student of ancient Rome the acquisition of skills is secondary to the understanding of a historical period. On the other hand when we speak of "teaching Spanish" or "studying French," presumably the student's goal is to learn to speak Spanish or read French. No doubt it is this ambiguity in the meaning of the terms "teach" and "study" that has led us to embrace new locutions in the field of religious studies and explains why we seldom use the term "learn." The prepositions "of" and "about" have not been admitted into our discourse without reflection. They dig a tiny moat between teacher and subject matter, signaling to ourselves and especially to others that there is a salutary distance between the teacher and what is taught. In the context of the modern university they make a necessary and useful distinction.

In an effort to put space between ourselves and the things we teach, however, we may have created an unbridgeable chasm. And it is for this reason that I invite you to consider another preposition, the "for" in the title of this address. If the prepositions "of" and "about" dig a moat between the teacher and subject matter, the preposition "for" casts a tiny drawbridge over the moat. Although it is possible to say "who speaks for religion?" the more concrete phrase "religious tradition" works better as the object of "for." It is easier to let down a drawbridge over the moat that separates scholar and subject matter if we speak about Buddhism or Christianity or Judaism or Islam, not the imagined "religion" that has its home only in the academy.

Now the preposition "for" is elusive. Like the terms "teach," "study," and "learn," its meaning fluctuates. To speak "for" a religious tradition may mean to be a spokesperson or an advocate for its beliefs and way of life. One answer then to the question "Who speaks for the religious traditions?" is bishops, ministers, imams, priests, lamas, and others who are the leaders and official representatives of the religions. But such an answer is imperfect and misleading, and deflects us from our topic. For though there are among us priests and rabbis and ministers and imams, we gather here as a company of scholars. It is to scholars that the question is addressed: "Who will speak *for* the religious traditions?"

So we must search for another sense to the preposition "for" than "on behalf of." My attention was first called to the importance of prepositions in religious studies in Wendy Doniger O'Flaherty's presidential address several years ago. She used the phrases "care for" and "care against." Just as she took some license in using the oxymoron "care against," I take some liberty in using "care for" as a way of rendering "for." She wrote: "Though it is deemed wrong to *care for* religion, it is not wrong to *care against* religion." Since the Enlightenment, "hatred of religion has been a more respectable scholarly emotion than love, particularly hatred of one's own religion."[3] What O'Flaherty calls hatred of religion is a picturesque way of portraying a familiar friend, critical reason, and the intellectual style it has fostered. Though most would eschew the emotional overtones of "hatred of religion," her observation is accurate. Criticism is the oxygen that quickens

3. Wendy Doniger O'Flaherty, "The Uses and Misuses of Other Peoples' Myths," *JAAR* 54 (1986): 230.

the academy. Without an analytic and inquiring disposition, without spirited skepticism and muscular toughmindedness, we would not be gathered together in this society as a company of scholars engaged in the study of religion in its kaleidoscope of forms and expressions.

It is, however, two hundred years since the Enlightenment lit up the dull sky of Western Europe. It has come time to ask whether "critical" reason as defined by the Enlightenment is the only intellectual trait we should honor, the only song we must sing. If "hatred" of one's own religion is a virtue, must love be a vice? To be sure, critical reason at its best is never "hostile" or "against," yet the Enlightenment taught us to esteem detachment (thereby excluding love), and in its wake it has been easy to identify critical thought with stepping back or stepping away from the object of our study as well as from inherited ways of thinking.

In his essay "What Is Enlightenment?" Immanuel Kant distinguished two roles of reason. The first he called public reason, the critical and analytical use of reason by a scholar before the reading public. The second he designated private reason, reason put at the service of religious or civil institutions.[4] In his view public reason alone bestowed enlightenment. Propelled by the spirit of free inquiry, it examined, tested, and criticized without regard to the dictates of others, that is, the official representatives of the religious institutions or of tradition. "Our age, is in especial degree, the age of criticism, and to criticism everything must submit."[5] Public reason was thought to be autonomous, private reason subject to a "self-incurred tutelage."

On the claim of liberating reason from its "tutelage" to authority, the Enlightenment sought a new public forum free of

4. Immanuel Kant, "What Is Enlightenment?" in *Foundations of the Metaphysics of Morals* (Indianapolis, 1959), 86-87.
5. Immanuel Kant, *Immanuel Kant's Critique of Pure Reason*, trans. Norman Kemp Smith (London, 1956), 9.

external constraints. This quest has met with uncommon success. Over the last two centuries, critical reason has not only won independence within society, it has created its own empire with peculiar institutions, traditions, language, and authorities. So profoundly has this new world altered the protocols of our intellectual life that one is minded to ask with George Steiner: "To what, save pride of intellect or professional peerage, is the reviewer, the critic, the academic expert accountable?"[6] Comfortable and content in its own home, "critical" reason is embarrassed to be associated with the very institutions it was expected to serve by its new freedom. For, according to Kant, one of the tasks of the public reason of the scholar was "to make suggestions for the better organization of the religious body. . . ."[7]

Within principles inherited from the Enlightenment, then, it is not out of place to ask whether other prepositions come into play in our scholarly life than "of" and "about." To be sure, no one preposition can define the many and varied relations that are formed in the life of a scholar and intellectual. Even the most single-minded among our company is tugged in several directions by reason of circumstances or sensibility. No thinking is wholly detached from its object; all thought stands in the midst of things seeking to correct or change course. Accordingly we must expand the repertoire of prepositions that define our common endeavor to include "for," in the admittedly imprecise sense of "care for." For too long we have assumed that engagement with the religious traditions is not the business of scholarship, as though the traditions will "care for" themselves. In the eighteenth century, when the weight of western Christian tradition lay heavily on intellectuals, there was reason to put distance between the scholar and the religious communities. Today that supposition is much less

6. George Steiner, *Real Presences* (Chicago, 1989), 8.
7. Kant, "What Is Enlightenment?" 88.

6

true and we must make place in our company for other scholarly virtues.

Of course, the vocation to "care for," however defined, will only be one task among many and one that applies most especially to students of the living religious traditions, and not of course to all students of these traditions. There are some in our company whose scholarly mission leads them along quite different paths. But that is hardly reason for all of us to approach "religion" as though it were the "creation of the scholar's study" or as if it existed only in the past. As Ernst Troeltsch reminds us, it makes a difference for an interpreter whether one is simply engaged in decently interring a corpse or dealing with a reality that has a future as well as a past.[8]

II

Whether one is speaking of the career of a politician, the value of a share on the stock market, the bond between estranged lovers, or the life of a religious idea, it makes a difference whether something has a future. The politician whose political life seemed at an end may be re-elected, the lovers who parted may find each other again, the religious idea may one day light the path of one's life. What has a future has life and can become part of *our* future. I was reminded of this several years ago shortly after I had moved to the University of Virginia. I was teaching a large survey course on medieval Christian history and a young woman came into my office to say she wanted to major in religious studies. Since I was new to Virginia, I was curious as to what drew her to our department. She told me she had been thinking for some time about

8. Ernst Troeltsch, *Writings on Theology and Religion*, ed. Robert Morgan and Michael Pye (Liverpool, 1977), 156-159.

her life after graduation, but it was not until the previous summer that she realized what she wanted to do. One morning while on vacation with her parents, she awoke and announced to her family: "I am going to major in religious studies and become a social worker!"

In the mind of this young woman the study of religion offered more than an understanding of another field of human knowledge. The stories she heard and the ideas she examined set in motion her own imaginings about the ends and purposes of human life, tacitly illuminating the choices she was making about the conduct of her life. Studies in religion spoke to her not only about the past or about what others say or do but about her future and what she might do and say. She was not simply a bystander. Translating her words into the vocabulary of classical antiquity, we might say that for her the study of religion was (among other things) a search for wisdom. And wisdom, not only in Western antiquity, but in other cultures as well, has always been a practical as well as a theoretical quest whose goals were moral and spiritual, not simply intellectual. In the words of Seneca, the Roman philosopher, wisdom's lessons are "not for the classroom but for life."[9]

Wisdom is an *ars vivendi,* hence the Romans spoke about *studium sapientiae.* The term "studium" is of course the root of our modern English word "study." However, the Latin *studium* does not mean "study" or "investigation" but a zealous pursuit or earnest quest. On occasion, the modern English term "study" carries these overtones, as in the vernacular expression "study war no more." Hence *studium sapientiae* is best translated with phrases that carry overtones of resolve and conviction, "pursuit of wisdom" or "zeal for wisdom." You will recall that when Augustine read Cicero's *Hortensius,* the book that planted in him the love

9. Seneca, *Ad Lucilium Epistulae Morales,* vol. 3, trans. Richard M. Gummere (Cambridge, 1971), 106.12.

of wisdom, it taught him not simply to "admire" this or that philosophy but to "love wisdom itself, to search for it, pursue it, hold fast to it, and embrace it firmly."[10]

Inevitably the study of religion, if it is not delivered into the hands of scholarly undertakers, has "sapiential" features, if not in the mind of the instructor, certainly in the mind of students. For the religious traditions speak about suffering, happiness, love, death, faith, doubt, hope, transcendence, enlightenment, appearance, reality, sin, reconciliation, wholeness, peace, the end of human life, God — in short about wisdom. The pursuit of wisdom can move the will and inflame the heart as well as excite the mind. There are reasons, then, why scholars and teachers shun the "sapiential" character of religious studies. The most obvious is the pluralism of our society (and our classrooms). The lecture podium is neither a *minbar* nor a pulpit, nor is the seminar room a *yeshiva*. Another reason is the broad interpretation our courts have given of the constitutional constraints on the establishment of religion. In this context it is understandable why the expression "teaching about religion" has gained currency in the academy. The impressive gains of recent years would not have been possible without fresh conceptions of the nature of religious scholarship. No one can be a member of a contemporary department of religious studies without appreciating how profoundly our intellectual life has been enriched by this new environment.

Nevertheless there have been losses. I can illustrate the point by an editorial that appeared in the *Washington Post* a year ago. The *Post* wrote: "The study of religion in the public school curriculum has always been an educational hot potato — even though, in contrast to unconstitutional religious practices in the schools, such as prayer, learning about religious traditions and conflicts is essential to understanding culture and history." The

10. Augustine, *Confessions,* trans. R. S. Pine-Coffin (Baltimore, 1964), 3.4.3.

9

editorial cites the recent proposal on teaching religion entitled "Living with our Deepest Differences." The premise of this program, opines the *Post*, is that one way to teach "about religion without offending sensibilities or the Constitution is to focus on the concepts of religious liberty and pluralism themselves."[11]

What first caught my attention in this editorial was of course the phrase "teaching about religion." (These prepositions have been rattling around in my head for some time.) I was also intrigued by the announcement of a new series for teaching religion in the schools with the superb and insightful title "Living with our Deepest Differences." The headline over the editorial, however, read "Teaching Religious Toleration," and this struck me as an odd way of putting things. For teaching religious toleration and teaching about religion are not the same thing. The confusion is not accidental. Teaching about religion, especially in the American context, is too easily translated into teaching about something else; and that is the subtle shift that takes place in this editorial. As the *Post* puts it, one way of teaching about religion is to "focus on concepts of religious liberty and pluralism." Here the teaching of religion is put at the service of instruction in the constitution, education in civic virtues, or a philosophical discussion of the principles of religious liberty. No matter how dear "religious liberty" and "pluralism" may be to a liberal society, they are hardly at the center of the great religious traditions (at least not until recently), and comprehending these principles will do little to help us understand our "deepest differences." The study of religion, it seems, can ignore the very things that religious people care about most deeply.

In a more sophisticated way similar assumptions undergird the scholarly study of religion in the university. In his fascinating

11. "Teaching Religious Toleration," *Washington Post*, October 22, 1988, A22.

book, simply entitled *Religion,* but with the subtitle, "If There Is no God. . . . On God, the Devil, Sin, and other Worries of the so-called Philosophy of Religion," Leszek Kolakowski addresses what he calls the epistemological foundation of the academic study of religious myths. Studies of the social, cognitive, or emotional value of myths imply that "the language of myth is translatable into a 'normal' language — which means, into one which is understandable within the semantic rules the researcher . . . is employing. . . . These codes help to disclose the hidden, 'profane' sense of mythical tales. . . ." Such study, continues Kolakowski, has two presuppositions. "First, it is assumed that myths, as they are explicitly told and believed, have a latent meaning behind their ostensible one and that this meaning not only is not in fact perceived by those sharing a given creed, but that of necessity it cannot be perceived. Secondly, it is implied that this latent meaning, which is accessible only to the outsider-anthropologist, is the meaning par excellence, whereas the ostensible one, i.e., the myth as understood by the believers, has the function of concealing the former. . . ."[12]

Strong words these. Perhaps Kolakowski overstates his point, but the target of his criticism is apparent. His choice of terms, particularly the phrase "ostensible meaning," is somewhat distracting, especially in a field where meaning is seldom stable and multiple senses are rife, yet the point is clear enough. The academy tolerates a linguistic hierarchy that subjugates religious discourse to the hegemony of a fictive outsider, to the "semantic rules of the researcher." We have welcomed into our midst a leveling contemporary idiom without roots in history or experience, a speech that is contrived, abstract, ephemeral. This is not to deny the necessity of studying the "latent" meaning of religious dis-

---

12. Leszek Kolakowski, *Religion: If There Is no God . . . On God, the Devil, Sin, and other Worries of the so-called Philosophy of Religion* (New York, 1982), 15.

course. In the last decades of the twentieth century it requires no great insight to recognize that the users of religious language say more than they intend, or more cynically, as much as they intend. But it does not take students of religion to see that. For that very reason Kolakowski's argument merits our attention. He alerts us to the tenacity of what I have called the "sapiential" features of religious language. In his words: "what people mean in religious discourse is what they ostensibly mean."[13]

In his recent book *Real Presences*, George Steiner addresses, from a quite different perspective, a like set of problems. He too is impatient with the "mandarin madness of secondary discourse" that "infects thought and sensibility," and he imagines, somewhat wistfully, a society "devoid, to the greatest possible extent of 'meta-texts,' this is to say, of texts about texts. . . ." Of course, if Steiner had his way most of us would be put out of business! The parallels to the study of religion are inexact. He is thinking of a city of poets, composers, painters, choreographers, and the like. Yet one of his purposes in writing the book was to rescue critical thinking from its domination by a "grey morass" of second order discourse, and to defend a view of criticism that makes place for engagement with the subject matter itself, for "ingestion," in Steiner's words, and which allows the interpreter to invest "his [or her] own being in the process of interpretation." Hence the play on the words "real" and "presence" in the title of his book. Genuine criticism makes "the past text a present presence," a living reality, and allows it to make claims on the future.[14]

What I draw from these three disparate illustrations, the editorial in the *Washington Post*, the passage from Kolakowski, and the remarks of George Steiner, is the following: if we allow the "ostensible" meaning of religious language to be taken hostage

---

13. Kolakowski, *Religion*, 16.
14. Steiner, *Real Presences*, 13.

to the etiquette of disinterested secondary discourse, or to things that have only a tangential relation to the things religious people care about, not only do we prune the list of things we talk about, we also narrow the circle of people we will talk to, or better, of those who will talk to us. And that is a great loss, a kind of self-imposed deafness. Where there is no one to answer, we are deprived of a precious intellectual gift — resistance. I am thinking not only of contemporaries. Let it not be forgotten that the great religions of the world are traditions of learning as well as of faith. Alongside of the practice of religion flourish lively intellectual traditions, philosophical, historical, exegetical, legal, created and nurtured for the purpose of understanding and interpreting the very things we study. Within the present intellectual climate it is easy, all too easy, to exclude from our circle of discourse the great scholars of the past, the likes of Maimonides or Averroes or Thomas Aquinas or Origen or Bukhari or Rashi. If the "ostensible" meaning of the myths and stories and doctrines is ancillary to the goals of the academic study of religion, we consign these thinkers to footnotes, transforming them into historical sources invoked for the purpose of documenting an idea or illustrating a theory. No longer welcomed as partners in a living dialogue, the lively voices of the dead fall silent as we turn our backs to them. The consequence is not only a loss of depth but also a sacrifice of memory.

III

At times it seems as though the ticket of admission to religious studies is a forfeiture of memory. And that is too high a price to pay. You may recall the touching scene at the end of *The Brothers Karamazov*. The boy Ilyusha has been buried and his friends are gathered at the grave. Alyosha speaks to them. "Let us agree here at Ilyusha's stone, never to forget, first, Ilyusha, and secondly, one another." He explains, "My dear children, perhaps you will not understand what I'm going to say to you now, for I often speak very incomprehensibly, but I'm sure, you will remember that there's nothing higher, stronger, more wholesome and more useful in life than some good memory. . . ." You are told a lot about education, he says, "but some beautiful, sacred memory, preserved since childhood, is perhaps the best education of all. If a [person] carries many such memories into life with him, he is saved for the rest of his life. And even if only one good memory is left in our hearts, it may also be the instrument of our salvation one day."[15]

Dostoevsky is speaking about personal memories. But all memory, even individual memory, rests on the communal experience of those who surround us, not on the private reminiscences of solitary persons, as the French social anthropologist Maurice Halbwachs has taught us. "A remembrance is gained not merely by reconstituting the image of a past event a piece at a time. That reconstruction must start from shared data or conceptions."[16] Cut off from collective memory it is easy for scholars to construct an entire framework of interpretation that has no relation to actual human experience or aspirations. We need to be reminded that scholarship on the living religious traditions cannot exist in isolation from the communities that are the bearers of these traditions, as though those who transmit and practice the things we study have no say, indeed no stake, in the interpretations we offer. This question was addressed rather effectively centuries ago in a dispute recorded in the Babylonian Talmud. The question arose about the role of the living tradition (the "oral law" in the language of

15. Fyodor Dostoevsky, *The Brothers Karamazov,* vol. 2, trans. David Magarshack (New York, 1974), 910-911.
16. Maurice Halbwachs, *The Collective Memory* (New York, 1980), 31.

the Talmud) in settling a dispute. If one ignores the "oral law," one teacher responded, it would be as though the Torah was "rolled up and left in a corner, and whoever wishes to study it can study it."[17] The metaphor is hauntingly apt in our scholarly milieu. The things we study, it is assumed, belong to no one; they are simply lying there waiting for whoever wishes to study them to study them and in whatever way one sees fit.

Without memory the language of scholarship is impoverished, barren, and lifeless, a tottering scaffold of secondary creations in which "words refer only to words."[18] If we keep a cool distance from temporality and history, we make the task of understanding more not less difficult. The image of stepping back is misleading if for no other reason than it assumes there is a place to step back to, as though we could grasp something on its own terms unrelated to who we are or where we stand.[19] Autonomy is not a pre-condition for understanding; quite the contrary, as reason penetrates more deeply into things its imaginative and critical powers are unleashed. Insofar as memory aids in this work, its role is not only prophylactic but constructive.

17. Kiddushin, *The Babylonian Talmud,* vol. 4, *Seder Naihim,* ed. I. Epstein (London, 1936), 66a.

18. The phrase is from Czeslaw Milosz's *The Witness of Poetry* (Cambridge, 1983), 49. He speaks there of the alienation of the poet from society, and the loss of a "community of beliefs and feelings which unite poet and audience" (65). In his Nobel Prize lecture he wrote: "Memory is our force; it protects us against a speech entwining upon itself like the ivy when it does not find a support on a tree or a wall" (*Nobel Lecture* [New York, 1980], 21).

19. See the interesting observations on this point by Johannes Fabian in *Time and the Other* (New York, 1983). Conceptions of time, he writes, are made "for the purpose of distancing those who are observed from the Time of the observer" (25). There is a "systematic tendency to place the referent(s) of anthropology in a Time other than the present of the producer of anthropological discourse" (31). On "stepping back" see Ricoeur: "Anyone who wished to escape the contingency of historical encounters and stand apart from the game in the name of a nonsituated 'objectivity' would at the most know everything, but would understand nothing" (Paul Ricoeur, *The Symbolism of Evil* [New York, 1967], 24).

In Kant's essay "What Is Enlightenment?" however, it was the liaison with tradition, with memory if you will, that obstructed the path to enlightenment. Affiliation with a particular tradition meant making a contract with an "unchangeable symbol" that "shut off all further enlightenment from the human race."[20] From this was drawn the conclusion: judgments and convictions derived from tradition or the shared history of a concrete community have no place in the public forum. In the marketplace of ideas, particular commitments are limiting and restrictive.

But is it really the case that identification with a particular tradition narrows the horizon of a scholar (any more than language or education or class or geography), or that it shuts one off from further enlightenment? Thirty years ago Hans-Georg Gadamer posed a similar question: "Does the fact that one is set within various traditions mean really and primarily that one is subject to prejudices and limited in one's freedom? Is not, rather, all human existence, even the freest, limited and qualified in various ways? If this is true, then the idea of an absolute reason is impossible for historical humanity. Reason exists for us only in concrete, historical terms . . . ."[21] If the leaden prose of *Truth and Method* is too dense, perhaps the same idea can be expressed in a more sprightly fashion by an aphorism of Cynthia Ozick. She said: "You have to blow through the narrow end of the shofar if you want to be heard far."[22]

20. Kant, "What Is Enlightenment?" 89.
21. Hans-Georg Gadamer, *Truth and Method* (New York, 1975), 245.
22. Cynthia Ozick, *Art and Ardor* (New York, 1984), 177.

IV

In the religious traditions I know best, Christianity, Judaism, and Islam, conviction and rational justification[23] have been complementary, seldom adversarial. The traditions preclude *mere* identification with themselves by presupposing general conditions of validity for their claims. The most impressive evidence for this is the readiness of religious thinkers to take their places in the public forum, subjecting their ideas to analysis, criticism, and correction, and testing their convictions by norms that are rooted within the tradition *and* by principles shared with other thoughtful people. Origen of Alexandria challenged his Greek critic Celsus to judge his views by the "common notions" that were accepted by other thinkers.[24] It was the Enlightenment, and historiography since that time, that promoted the idea that "traditional" religion was based solely on "faith" independent of the claims of reason. "The great religions of antiquity," it was said, "all bear this character: they were not reasoned about; they did not require proof and hence could not be disproved."[25]

As I have already observed, the great religious traditions of the world are not only communities of "faith," they are also traditions of learning. Now the phrase "tradition of learning" can mean several things depending on which religious tradition one has in mind. For the "civilizational religions" it means at least that books have been one of the media of transmission, and the reading of old books has often been the agent of change

23. On the conflict between conviction and rational justification, see Alasdair MacIntyre, *Whose Justice? Which Rationality?* (Notre Dame, 1988), 6.

24. Origen, *Origen: Contra Celsum,* trans. Henry Chadwick (Cambridge, 1965), 3.40.

25. Peter Gay, *The Enlightenment: An Interpretation,* vol. 1, *The Rise of Modern Paganism* (New York, 1967), 90.

and innovation. Judah ha-Nasi codified the Jewish laws in the Mishnah, the Amoraiim read the Mishnah, and their debates are recorded in the Talmud; Rashi and the Tosaphists commented on their discussions; and later editions of the Talmud incorporate all these opinions in the margins of the text so that the contemporary student can enter into a discussion that has been going on for centuries. Because books are foundational, all the activities associated with the transmission and interpretation of books have occupied a large place in the intellectual agenda of these traditions: the copying of manuscripts, the study of grammar, the analysis of words and concepts, the writing of commentaries.

Religious scholarship, however, has never been simply a matter of copying texts, of parsing sentences, of analyzing and explaining words and phrases. It has always been a work of *critical* intelligence. Peter Abelard wrote: "For the first key to wisdom is called *interrogation,* diligent and unceasing questioning. . . . By doubting we are led to inquiry; and from inquiry we perceive the truth." Abelard surely believed the biblical maxim, "the fear of the Lord is the beginning of wisdom," nevertheless he begins with "questioning," even doubt. To support this view he first cites Aristotle: "In doubting we come to investigation and in investigating we perceive the truth." Then he quotes a saying of Jesus of Nazareth: "Seek and ye shall find." Even as a child, according to Abelard, Jesus understood the importance of questioning in the quest for wisdom. When he was taken to the temple with his parents Jesus questioned the learned doctors of the Law. Whether biblical scholars will applaud Abelard's exegetical inventiveness is not our business; Abelard believed that he had found warrant for his theological method in the example of Jesus.

Abelard's observations on doubt and questioning are taken

from his book *Sic et Non.*[26] This work was a collection of traditional authorities arranged according to a catalogue of philosophical, theological, and moral topics. What gave the book its pungency was that it offered opinions on either side of each issue; some writers said *"sic"* and others said *"non."* In the course of the book Abelard was able to display notable differences among Christian thinkers on key points of faith and morals. The form of the book is unique in the Middle Ages, but the principles that underlie it were commonplace; for medieval thinkers, the path to enlightenment led necessarily through rigorous and relentless questioning.

I choose my illustrations from the Middle Ages because that is one period in the history of our civilization when Christianity, Judaism, and Islam engaged in lively and fruitful religious dialogue with each other. The Middle Ages may be called an "age of faith," but its most original thinkers seldom spoke solely to members of their own communities. Often their discussions were three-cornered, or perhaps one should say four-cornered, because the intellectual impetus for religious and philosophical thought came from Aristotle, whose works, read by Muslims, Jews, and Christians alike, presented the three traditions with a common set of problems. Muslim philosophers had translated Aristotle into Arabic, and Maimonides, who lived in Cairo, first read Aristotle in Arabic. These Arabic versions were in turn translated into Latin and read by Albert Magnus, Thomas Aquinas' teacher, in Paris and Cologne. As Maimonides' ideas became known in the West his books were translated into Latin. Without Maimonides' philosophical rationale for the proofs of the exis-

26. *Sic et Non* has not been translated into English. For the passage discussed here, see Blanche B. Boyer and Richard McKeon, *Peter Abailard Sic et Non: A Critical Edition* (Chicago, 1976), 103-104.

tence of God or his defense of a temporal creation, Thomas' task would have been immensely more difficult. Conversely, Thomas Aquinas' synthesis of faith and reason made it easier for Jewish thinkers in Western Europe to respond to the arguments of Averroes. Hillel of Verona, a contemporary of Thomas, translated his *De unitate Intellectus* into Hebrew for the purpose of answering Averroes' attack on the idea of personal immortality. In the fifteenth century Joseph Albo, a Jewish philosopher living in Spain, drew on the works of Thomas to offer a reasoned presentation of Judaism.[27]

Now before I become mired too deeply in medieval intellectual history, let me return to the point of these observations. In saying that the civilizational religions are traditions of learning as well as of faith, I mean that they have fostered a critical spirit, and that the ideas they have embraced and the doctrines they have confessed, as well as the stories they have told, have been the subject of rational and philosophical scrutiny for centuries, not only by those within the traditions but also by outsiders. Religious convictions do not operate outside of warrants in use in other areas of thought and experience. Augustine wrote long ago: "No one believes anything unless one first thought it to be believable. . . . Everything which is believed should be believed after thought has preceded. . . . Not everyone who thinks believes, since many think in order not to believe; but everyone who believes thinks . . ." (*pred. sanct.* 2.5).[28] Religious convic-

---

27. In the introduction to his classical study of Thomas Aquinas, Gilson wrote: "Christian thought, Jewish thought, and Musulman thought acted and reacted on each other as we know, and it would not be at all satisfactory to study them as so many closed and isolated systems" (*The Spirit of Mediaeval Philosophy* [New York, 1940], 1).

28. English translation of "On the Predestination of the Saints *(pred. sanct.)*," in *Nicene and Post-Nicene Fathers,* ed. Philip Schaff, First Series, vol. 5 (Grand Rapids, 1956), pp. 493-520.

tions, to use a Buddhist phrase I have learned from my colleague Jeffrey Hopkins, are based on "valid cognition."

Let us then make place in our company for those who come toting their shofars or trumpets or french horns or tubas — they will make our assembly a more tuneful gathering. There is no reason for the scholar as scholar to shed her or his convictions to exercise the vocation of scholar. No doubt there are fields in which one's religious convictions may appear irrelevant or intrusive (in the social scientific study of religion for example), but in other fields that is surely not the case. We have created, it seems, an intellectual climate that discourages, if not prohibits, the scholar from speaking as a member of a religious community. We continue to perpetrate the eighteenth-century view that religion is "inevitably sectarian,"[29] or the more recent notion that faith designates a private world of feelings and emotions impenetrable to the outsider. But fideism, though it may be rife in certain circles, is a caricature of the great religious traditions of the world. Rationality is not synonymous with detachment, and particular commitments can be the vehicle of enlightenment, as Flannery O'Connor shrewdly observed: "There is no reason why fixed dogma should fix anything that the writer sees in the world. On the contrary, dogma is an instrument for penetrating reality."[30]

V

Until a generation ago most religious scholarship took place within institutions affiliated with the religious traditions, in seminaries and

29. The phrase is from the Rockfish Gap Report written by Thomas Jefferson. Martin E. Marty, "Committing the Study of Religion in Public," *JAAR* 57 (1989): 1.

30. Flannery O'Connor, *Mystery and Manners* (New York, 1957), 178.

divinity schools, in rabbinical colleges and yeshivas, and in madresehs. Within a very short time, in this country, and to a growing
extent elsewhere in the world, scholarship in the field of religion has
shifted to the colleges and universities. The department of which I
am a member now has twenty-two members; twenty-five years ago
it had one member. To be sure the universities and colleges are not
the only centers of religious scholarship; outstanding scholars on
whose work we all depend are found in theological schools and
seminaries. Unfortunately, within the profession there is a pervading
sense that the community that matters is the university.

There can be no doubt that this move to the university has
been a great boon for scholarship in the field of religion. In the
course of its history religious scholarship has had many homes:
the talmudic academies, the monastic universities of Tibet, the
cathedral schools and monasteries in medieval Europe, seminaries
and divinity schools, the madresehs. Even within specific traditions the setting of religious scholarship has peregrinated. In the
early centuries of Islam, learning was transmitted wholly through
individual teachers and informal discussion, often in the courts
of the wealthy where learned men were "thrust into each other's
presence by a bored or curious monarch."[31] Students wandered
from place to place seeking out a teacher, learning what he had
to offer, then moving on to another teacher. In time this practice
was displaced by the "madreseh," a formal school located at a
particular place organized around a company of scholars, a uni-
form curriculum, and of course fixed fees and paid teachers. These
schools generated a whole new range of intellectual concerns, for
example, treatises on logic, and later, works on philosophy.

As the establishment of madresehs within Islam had unfore-

31. Roy Mottahedeh, *The Mantle of the Prophet: Religion and Politics in Iran*
(New York, 1985), 89.

seen yet fruitful consequences for the development of Islamic thought, so the move to the university has invigorated scholarship within many religious traditions. Whether one points to the acquisition of new philological skills, to awareness of social factors in religious history, to demythologizing of religious ideology, to sophistication about questions of method, to more intimate acquaintance with the religious traditions of the East, there can be no doubt that the academy offers opportunities for scholarship in religion that are without precedent in the history of religions.

Nevertheless, as the prepositions "of" and "about" signify, the academic study of religion has altered the relation between the scholar and the thing studied in subtle ways. Prepositions, as I noted at the outset, have to do with relations, and it would be a great loss for the university and the society (as well as the religions themselves) if scholarship on the learned religious traditions was tolerated only within the astringent precincts prescribed by the "study of religion" and "teaching about religion." If love is no virtue and there is no love of wisdom, if religion can only be studied from afar and as though it had no future, if the passkey to religious studies is amnesia, if we can speak about our deepest convictions only in private, our entire enterprise is not only enfeebled, it loses credibility. For if those who are engaged in the study of religion do not care for religion, should others? Without "living sympathy" and a "certain partisan enthusiasm," Goethe once wrote to Schiller, "there is so little value in our utterance that it is not worth making at all. Pleasure, delight, sympathy with things is what alone is real and what in turn creates reality; all else is worthless and only detracts from the worth of things."[32]

32. J. W. Goethe, *Selections from the Correspondence Between Schiller and Goethe,* ed. J. G. Robertson (Boston, 1898), 33.

2

Religious Pluralism and Early Christian Thought

IT IS I SUPPOSE one task of the historical theologian to remind others that issues debated in our time have been the subject of intellectual scrutiny in earlier times. In many theological questions — for example, faith and reason, providence, theodicy, Christology, Trinity — this is self-evident, and it is customary in works of theology to retrace earlier debates and arguments. In the present discussion of religious pluralism, however, little place is given to earlier sources that deal with the topic. That is due, I suspect, to the assumption that our age is unique, and that the "problem" of religious pluralism has moved to the head of the agenda because of social and religious developments in the twentieth century, notably the extensive and enduring contacts between the major religious traditions of the world. Certainly that is the impression one gains from reading the growing body of literature on the topic; most books begin with a statement of our new historical situation and the challenges it provides for theology. "The time has indeed come for members of the Christian

Originally published in *Pro Ecclesia* 1, no. 1 (1992): 89-103. Reprinted with permission.

community to face the challenges — theological, intellectual, and moral — posed by their increasing awareness of the religious diversity of humankind."[1]

Christians, however, have long had to face the challenge of other religions. For the first four hundred years of Christian history a traditional religious culture (which was not, as once thought, moribund) set the agenda for many Christian intellectuals, and its spokesmen energetically contested what seemed to be the pretensions of the new religion. Since the seventh century a large part of the Christian world, Christians residing in the Eastern Mediterranean, for example, in Egypt, Syria, and Iraq, have lived in the face of the seemingly invincible presence of Islam, and at a later date Christians in the great Orthodox capital of Constantinople, as well as those in Greece, Bulgaria, and neighboring regions, had to adjust to life under the rule of Ottoman Turks. Even in the Middle Ages, once thought to be a period of Christian spiritual as well as political hegemony, Western Christian thinkers were challenged by the continued vitality of Jewish communities in their midst and by the boldness of Islamic philosophy. What is different today, I suspect, is not that Christianity has to confront other religions, but that we now call this situation "religious pluralism." For behind the term "religious pluralism" lurks not so much a question as an answer, the view that particular traditions cannot be the source of ultimate truth. All religions, it is assumed, are culturally conditioned responses to the mystery of the divine and cannot be the criterion for

1. Donald G. Dawe and John B. Carman, *Christian Faith in a Religiously Plural World* (New York, 1978), 1. See also John Hick, *Problems of Religious Pluralism* (New York, 1985), 101; survey of recent literature by Francis X. Clooney, "Christianity and World Religions: Religion, Reason, and Pluralism," *RSR* 15 (1989): 197-204; and Paul Knitter, "Making Sense of Many," *RSR* 15 (1989): 204-209. For another view see J. A. DiNoia, *The Diversity of Religions* (Washington, D.C., 1992).

determining how others (who are not part of one's culture or tradition) should worship and serve God.

What has struck me in reading through some of the recent literature on "religious pluralism" is how little is said about earlier Christian thinkers who discussed the matter. No doubt that reflects in part a presumption that runs throughout nineteenth- and twentieth-century theology, namely, that critical thought has made a quantum leap beyond the assumptions of the earlier philosophical and theological tradition, and that theology, with impunity, can do its work without reference to the classical sources. In the case of religious pluralism, however, this conventional bias seems to have been intensified. So my task will be first to show why earlier Christian thinkers challenged the assumptions undergirding "religious pluralism," and then to draw out the implications for our present discussion.

The Problem of Relativism

The oldest and most enduring criticism of Christianity is an appeal to religious pluralism. Its classical statement was the *Relatio* (Report) of Symmachus, the Roman senator, to the Roman Emperor Valentinian in 384 concerning the Altar of Victory in the senate house in Rome. In the face of what he took to be Christian exclusivism, Symmachus defended a genial toleration of differing ways to the divine. "We gaze at the same stars, the sky belongs to all, the same universe surrounds us. What difference does it make by whose wisdom someone seeks the truth? We cannot attain to so great a mystery by one road" (PL 16.1010).

Symmachus was not the first to give voice to these sentiments. In much the same language, an earlier critic of Christianity, Porphyry, the disciple of Plotinus, had mounted arguments against the presumed exclusivism of Christianity. Porphyry was offended by the words of Jesus in the Gospel of John: "I am the way, and the truth, and the life; no one comes to the Father but by me" (John 14:6). He comments, "If Christ says he is the way, the grace, and the truth, and claims that only in himself can believing souls find a way to God, what did the people who lived in the many centuries before Christ do . . . ?" (in Augustine, *ep.* 102.8). In Porphyry's view, it was arrogant for Christians to think that men and women have had access to God only since the coming of Christ. "No teaching," he writes, "has yet been established which offers a *universal* way for the liberation of the soul" (*civ. dei* 10.32).[2]

But there was yet an earlier stage in this controversy, the debate between Celsus, the Greek intellectual, and Origen of Alexandria. Celsus had written a book entitled *True Doctrine (Alethes Logos)* in the latter part of the second century (ca. 175-180 C.E.), and Origen, when he was at the height of his intellectual powers (ca. 246 C.E.), wrote a massive response to Celsus in eight books. The *True Doctrine* is an impressive work, based on first-hand knowledge of Christian life and practices and on study of the Christian Scriptures. Celsus writes not simply as a rootless intellectual, but as an ardent defender of the traditional piety, institutions, and beliefs that marked the life of the cities of the Roman Empire. Celsus believed that Christianity was a revolt against practices that had served the peoples of the Mediterranean world for centuries. By making the divine accessible in ritual, custom, law, and story, these ancient traditions had given purpose and direction to communities and meaning to the lives of individuals, and Celsus could see no reason why the accumulated wisdom and experience of centuries should be abandoned in favor of a religion that was born only a few generations earlier. For

2. For discussion of pagan criticism of Christianity in antiquity see Robert L. Wilken, *The Christians as the Romans Saw Them* (New Haven, 1984). For early Christian discussion of "religion" see G. Vallée, "Le Lieu Patristique d'une Theologie des Religions," *Science et Esprit* 28 (1976): 55-64.

Celsus the "ancient doctrine" was the "true doctrine" (*Cels.* 1.14); Christianity promoted a form of piety grounded in neither antiquity nor tradition.[3]

Celsus realized of course that practices and beliefs varied from place to place. The peoples of the world had followed different customs not only with respect to dress, food, agriculture, husbandry, sex, and architecture but also with respect to the gods. By the second century of the common era educated people like Celsus were well traveled and informed about the differences between Egypt and Greece, Syria and North Africa, Asia Minor and Rome. Like their modern counterparts, intellectuals traveled the world seeking the wisdom, as well as the adulation, of men and women in foreign parts; they had also read Herodotus who had traveled to Egypt, to Syria, and to Mesopotamia as well as to Italy and other parts of Greece. Herodotus filled the pages of his work with vivid descriptions of the ways other people lived. In Egypt he reported that priests shave their heads, whereas among most other peoples priests grow their hair long; Egyptians live with their animals, knead bread with their feet, write from right to left, circumcise, drink from brass cups, and wear linen clothing, and on and on. Some people, Herodotus reported, venerate crocodiles, others practice cannibalism, and yet others worship snakes; and each nation seemed to consider a different kind of animal fit for sacrifice, some refused to sacrifice sheep, others shunned cows, and yet others abhorred the pig.

For the ancients the differences in customs and beliefs were felt most keenly in the realm of morality. In book 3 of Cicero's *De Republica*, Philus asks: Is *justitia* determined by a particular community's traditions, that is, is it a matter of laws established by a city *(civile)*, or is it grounded in nature? The argument is put forth that

---

3. Text of *Contra Celsum* in Marcel Borret, ed., *Origéne: Contra Celse*, 5 vols. (Paris, 1967-76). ET Henry Chadwick, *Origen: Contra Celsum* (Cambridge, 1965).

justice, unlike heat or cold, bitter or sweet, cannot be a matter of nature, because if that were so "justice and injustice would be the same thing to all people" (*Rep.* 3.8.13). If one visits different nations, one discovers that in Egypt a bull is considered divine; in Greece, as in Rome, one finds that there are statues of gods in human form, something which the Persians condemn. Other peoples, for example, Taurians on the Black Sea and Gauls and Carthaginians, believe that human sacrifices are an act of piety. Furthermore, not only is there diversity from place to place, but within a single city there have been "a thousand changes" in customs over the course of time. As illustration, Philus, with uncanny prescience, mentions changes in the rights of women (*iura mulierum*) concerning inheritance. "Why," he asks, "should a woman not have money of her own (i.e., be able to receive an inheritance)?"

If it was God "who had provided laws for us," so the argument continues, "then all people would observe the same laws, and the same people would not have had different laws at different times." Given this diversity of practices, the good and just person is faced with a dilemma. "Must one obey all the laws that exist?" (3.9.18). The conclusion seems inevitable: justice is not grounded in nature but in convention. In the *True Doctrine* Celsus uses this same reasoning, as well as some of the same examples, to make his case against the Christians. Other thinkers had resisted the implications of this argument; Plato, for example, had argued that virtue is not simply the opinion of the city (*Laws* 890d), but Celsus is not troubled by "relativism." He acknowledges that customs differ from place to place, and that present practices "happen to have been established" and "fixed by common consent," yet he asserts that custom is binding ("custom is king," in the words of Pindar).[4] "It is impious," he says, "to abandon those

4. *Celsus* 5.34. Words of Pindar found in frg. 49, A. Puech, ed., *Pindare*, vol. 4 (Paris, 1923), 118.

customs which have existed in a particular place from the beginning." Hence one must "preserve" what has been established by those who have gone before (5.25). Celsus is a consummate multi-culturalist.

Origen responds initially with ridicule: Is it right, he asks, for the Scythians to practice parricide, or for the Persians to allow mothers to marry their sons or fathers their daughters? Let Celsus explain how it is "impious" to break such laws! If one follows Celsus' argument it is pious to offer children for sacrifice to the gods. In Celsus' view piety, that is, true religion, "will not be divine by nature, but a matter of arbitrary arrangement and opinion; for among some people it is pious to worship the crocodile and to eat some animal worshipped by others, and among others it is pious to worship the calf. . . . Thus the same person will be making things to be pious by the standard of one set of laws and impious by another, which is the most ridiculous thing of all" (5.27).[5]

The difficulty with Celsus' view, says Origen, is that he is "confused in his conception of the nature of justice." For if justice and piety and holiness are "relative" (Greek for this is *pros ti*) and the same action can be pious or impious "under differing conditions," then it follows not only that justice is relative but also that the other virtues, temperance, courage, and wisdom, are relative. And again Origen concludes, "nothing could be more absurd than this."

Origen is as unoriginal as Celsus. His argument against Celsus' relativism had been worked out centuries earlier. In debates with the Epicureans Chrysippus had argued that "justice is a matter of nature not convention." From this he drew the con-

---

5. For discussion of relativity of moral ideas in antiquity see William A. Banner, "Origen and the Tradition of Natural Law Concepts," *Dumbarton Oak Papers* 8 (1954): 51-82.

clusion that virtue is grounded in nature, and to live virtuously is to live according to nature. Hence justice is not bound to a particular people or city; it is universal and can be known irrespective of who one is and where one lives.

Origen the Theologian

But it is not as a philosopher that Origen claims our attention. His philosophical response to Celsus follows a well-worn path. Just as the reader thinks he is about to leave the topic, however, Origen launches on a new and quite different line of reasoning, now theological rather than philosophical. What makes the argument interesting, as well as original, is that it rests on the necessary bond between Christianity and Judaism, a linkage that Celsus had exploited in his rebuttal of Christianity (7.18; 3.5; 4.2).

According to Origen, as well as Celsus, one way of accounting for the variety of customs among the peoples of the world is that the world had been divided up into regions and each territory had been assigned a different overseer who led people along different paths. Origen gives this view a biblical interpretation by pointing to the passages in the Torah that speak of God dividing the nations, for example, Deuteronomy 32:8-9. The text from Deuteronomy, however, does not simply speak of the "nations," it speaks specifically about the people of Israel: "The Lord's portion was Jacob his people, Israel the lot of his inheritance."

To give flesh to his argument Origen presents an elaborate interpretation of the scattering of the nations of the world after the building of the tower of Babel. As the nations moved away from the place where the tower was built, they lost sight of the light that once shone on them. Led by a guardian angel, each moved to a new region and even learned a new language. Only the Jews stayed in the "east" and did not forget the "eastern language" (*Cels.* 5.31). Origen is speaking about the election of the Jewish people.

Celsus had criticized the Jews because they had maintained their own law "as though they had some deeper wisdom." In their ignorance (thinking their doctrine was unique rather than derivative) they turned away from the society of the nations. In response Origen grants Celsus' point: the Jews do consider themselves "an elect portion of the supreme God preferred before any other nation" (5.42). But he does more; he defends the election of the Jews by an appeal to Jewish practice. If one were to "compare them with the way of life of other peoples, one would admire none more, since as far as it is humanly possible they have repudiated what is valueless to humankind [in the worship of God], and accepted only what is good."

In effect, Origen says to Celsus: if you want to appeal to ethnography to show that it matters little what people practice (whether they worship a crocodile or a bull), I will appeal to ethnography to show you that what they practice does make a difference. For it is not enough to ask whether certain practices are venerable or traditional or whether they bind together a community, but one must ask whether they foster worship of the one true God. Ethnography has no privileged status in matters of religious truth; the ways of the nations must be evaluated in light of our knowledge of God. "What an admirable thing it was for [the Jews] that they were taught even from childhood to rise above all sensible nature and not to think that God is established in any part of it, but even to seek for him beyond material things." Because of their way of life "they deserve to be called God's portion" (5.43). The Jews *do* "possess some deeper wisdom" because they do not "fall down to idols and daemons, and even the lowliest Jew looks only to the God of all." Plato, the great teacher of the Greeks, was not nearly as successful as Moses and his successors in training a people to be "devoted to God."

Celsus had charged that the Jews were runaway slaves from Egypt and contributed nothing new to humankind. But, says Origen, if we study their "society in their early days when the law was given, one would find that [the Jews] were people who manifested a shadow of the heavenly life upon earth." How do we know this? "Because among them none was regarded as God other than the supreme God, and none of those who made images possessed citizenship. There were no painters or image-makers in their society, since the law banished from it any people of this sort, in order that there might be no occasion for the making of images which takes hold of unintelligent people and drags the eyes of their soul down from God to earth" (*Cels*. 4.31).

Nothing, however, in human nature is "permanent," says Origen, and there came a time when "[the Jewish] way of life needed to be changed so that it was suitable for people everywhere." This change took place at the time of Jesus. His "noble religion" was given to those who believe "in all places," not just in one land and among one people. What Jesus taught, however, was the same as what the Jews taught. "He overthrew the teaching about the daemons on earth, who delight in frankincense and blood and the odours rising from burnt sacrifices, and drag men down from the *true conception of God* . . ." (4.32). Through Jesus the Jewish way of worshipping God reached out beyond the Jews and became accessible to all peoples.

How does one come to the true conception of God? Origen argues that our conception of God begins with the naming of God. Celsus had said that "it makes no difference whether we call Zeus the Most High, or Zen, or Adonai, or Sabaoth, or Amoun like the Egyptians, or Papaeus like the Scythians" (*Cels*. 5.45).[6] But, says

6. Hick: "Divine Reality exceeds the reach of our earthly speech and thought.

Origen, names are not "arbitrary conventions." They cannot be indiscriminately exchanged. Names have power, and when one translates a name from one language to another it loses its authority. If this is so with respect to human names, it is even more true with respect to the name of God. The proper name for God, says Origen, is "the God of Abraham and the God of Isaac and the God of Jacob." This name cannot be replaced by other names; indeed it is not possible to translate the "God of Abraham, Isaac, and Jacob" as though one could replace the name with its "meaning." For example, it would be ludicrous to name God "the God of the chosen father of the echo" (Philo's interpretation of Abraham), or "the God of laughter" (based on the meaning of Isaac), or "the God of the man who strikes with the heel [again, Philo on Jacob]."[7] This is why Moses and the prophets prohibit people from "naming the name of other gods with a mouth that has been trained to pray to the one God over all, and from remembering them with a heart that is taught to be free from all vanity of thought and speech" (*Cels.* 5.46). Zeus and Sabaoth are not identical.

Behind names, then, are found different conceptions of God; hence the place to begin speaking about the nature of God is with the name. Pluralism in the naming of God is evidence that people "have given up the pure idea of the Creator of the universe" (6.39). Therefore Celsus' defense of the theological integrity of pluralism has to be rejected. The existence of different ways of worship and different names of God is not an argument against the worship of the true God.

The name of God must be learned from God's "appearance"

It cannot be encompassed in human concepts. It is infinite, eternal, limitlessly rich beyond the scope of our finite conceiving of experience. Let us then both avoid the particular names used within the particular traditions and yet use a term which is consonant with the faith of each of them — ultimate Reality, or the Real."

7. On Abraham, see Philo *de gig.* 64; on Isaac, *leg. alleg.* 1.82; and on Jacob, *leg. alleg.* 1.61.

(*Cels.* 3.14), not from human experience or speculation or accumulated wisdom. Celsus had said that Plato (in his seventh epistle) had spoken about a "first good" (or the highest good), which comes to human beings "from long familiarity" with the "highest good" by a light "like a flame in the soul kindled by a leaping spark." Origen believes that in this passage, Celsus, with the help of Plato, had finally gotten things right, for knowledge of the "first good" comes about because "God *revealed* these things to [human beings]. . . ." If this is so, it is possible to make judgments about whether certain conceptions or practices are "worthy of God" (*Cels.* 6.3).

Here is the nub of Origen's argument. Because of "what is called in the Bible God's descent into human affairs" (4.14), it is now clear that certain forms of piety, certain religious observances, certain theological conceptions are "unworthy" of God, and that others, to use a term from later Greek theology, are *theoprepes,* befitting God. On this basis Origen subjects Celsus' views to criticism. By justifying animal sacrifices and upholding the adoration of images of marble and wood, Celsus dishonored the very God whose worship he championed. By acknowledging that one could properly worship God by venerating lesser deities (e.g., daimones and stars), Celsus remains wedded to the earth, his eyes trained not on the God of the universe but on "images and human statues unable to advance to the worship of the creator" (*Cels.* 5.35).

For Origen, as for other early Christian thinkers, religion was a matter of seeing,[8] and in this he is faithful to one of the central themes of the Scriptures. God is "seen," writes Origen,

---

8. Faith's goal, writes Augustine, is "ineffabilis pulchritudo, cuius plena *visio* est summa felicitas" (*Enchirion* 5). On the importance of light in Origen's epistemology, see John Dillon, "The Knowledge of God in Origin," in *Knowledge of God in the Graeco-Roman World,* ed. R. van dan Broek, T. Baarda, and J. Mansfeld (Leiden, 1988), 219-228.

"not only in the way implied in the words 'Blessed are the pure in heart for they shall see God,' but also in the way implied in the saying of the Image of the invisible God that 'He who has seen me has seen the Father who sent me'" (John 14:9; Col. 1:15; *Cels.* 7.42). The God who was beyond comprehension, who was not bound to time and space, had become known through things that could be seen. In debating the merits of differing religious practices, Origen insisted over and over again that the issue is not whose experience was more legitimate or authentic, but whether one had seen what God had revealed to humankind. Celsus had claimed that Christians had no "sure foundation" for their belief, to which Origen responded: we make no claim about a presumed foundation, our claim is based on "divine action" *(theias energeias)*, for "its origin is God who taught men by the prophets." Our teaching is not the product of "human sagacity" (3.14).[9]

That God "existed within the compass of that man who appeared in Judea" (*princ.* 2.6.2) was for Origen the central "divine action." Citing John 1:18, "No one has seen God at any time; the only begotten God who is in the bosom of the Father, he has declared him," he comments: "[Christ] revealed to his true disciples the nature of God and told them about His characteristics" (2.71).[10] Yet it is noteworthy that Origen never presents the appearance of God in Christ without reference to the appearances of God in Israel. It was the same God who "established Judaism in the first place, and later Christianity" (3.14).

In their writings to the cultured despisers of Christianity, the early Christian apologists, like apologists in every age, singled out those points of Christian belief that were readily intelligible to the

---

9. Elsewhere Origen writes: "But we affirm that human nature is not sufficient in any way to seek for God and to find him in his pure nature, unless it is helped by the God who is object of the search" (7.42).

10. This text, much beloved by early Christian thinkers, is cited in the first paragraph of John of Damascus' work, *Of the Orthodox Faith.*

cultural world they inhabited. In restating the Christian doctrine of God within the Graeco-Roman world, Christian thinkers sought out points of contact between biblical language of God's transcendence and Greek philosophical conceptions of the nature of God. Like others, Origen argued that "the doctrines of our faith are in complete accord with common notions" shared by philosophers and other thoughtful people. As we have seen, Origen's first line of defense against Celsus' relativism is to appeal to such common notions by restating an old argument about the nature of justice. Christians did not make private appeals to faith or claim privileged access to God; they cheerfully entered the marketplace of ideas.

Yet, in his reply to Celsus on the matter of religious pluralism, Origen does not rest his case, finally, on an appeal to philosophical principles.[11] Instead he introduces a rather elaborate historical argument based on the events of Christ's life and on the history of Israel and the religious practices of the Jewish people. Which is to say he thought that the "facts" of biblical history had a place in public discussions with non-Christians, namely with his Greek critic Celsus.

How could this be? For one thing Origen thought that the events of biblical history, like other stories purporting to relate past events, were not accepted on faith. Their historicity was open to critical scrutiny. While granting that it is difficult to "substantiate almost any story as historical fact," he argued that the "narrative about Jesus in the Gospels" is reliable (*Cels.* 1.42ff.).[12] Further, throughout the *Contra Celsum* Origen links his appeal

11. Of course there was also a philosophical transaction in the works of the early apologists, and they embraced certain ideas which were known independently of historical revelation. Yet their appropriation of the philosophical tradition was critical, informed by biblical history. See Wolfhart Pannenberg, "The Appropriation of the Philosophical Concept of God as a Dogmatic Problem of Early Christian Theology," in *Basic Questions in Theology,* vol. 2 (Philadelphia, 1971), 119-183.

12. See also *Celsus* 2.56.

to God's appearance in Christ to the existence of a new community composed of men and women whose lives have been changed and who offer true worship to God (*Cels.* 1.31 passim). The "fact" of the church, that is, the evidence of its life and worship, like the testimony provided by Jewish worship of the one God, is integral to his argument against Celsus.

Origen is convinced that what he has learned from Jewish history and the revelation in Christ, as well as from Jewish and Christian practice, has given him criteria by which to discern what worship befits God. He is willing to criticize certain forms of piety as unworthy of God. Celsus, says Origen, had trained his eyes not on the "God of all," but on "images and human statues, not wanting to advance in devotion to the creator" (5.35). From Origen's perspective, Celsus upheld forms of piety that were incompatible with God's nature and character. Jesus and Moses, on the other hand, directed human beings solely to the God of all, not to tribal or national deities, to the one supreme God, not to intermediary beings (4.32). In singling out the revelation in Israel and in Christ, Origen wishes to point his readers to a way of life that is open to all.

As one sifts through Origen's arguments, it becomes apparent that he is offering a theological critique of religion. In his view many of the practices of his contemporaries did not lift the soul to the true God, the God of all. Only certain forms of worship are pleasing to God. If people offer God lesser oblations, they demean and diminish God's glory; and if they call upon God using another name, they are not addressing the true God.

Porphyry and St. Augustine

Origen's defense of Christianity against Celsus prompted another defense of the traditional religion. At the end of the third century Porphyry wrote a book entitled *Philosophy from Oracles,* which compiled religious lore from many peoples of the ancient world. His ostensible aim was to discover a way of approaching God that was universal, that embraced all peoples and times and places, that transcended the particular traditions of the cities and the many peoples of the Mediterranean world. By his own admission his quest was unsuccessful. He did not find such a way, for by definition historical events could not be the source of ultimate truth. Like Celsus, his solution to the dilemma was to defend the traditional ways of the various nations and to identify genuine religion with the traditions of one's ancestors. In a letter written to his wife Marcella, whom he had married late in life to have spiritual children (so he said) not children by the flesh, he said: "The greatest fruit of piety is to worship the gods according to the traditions of one's ancestors" (*Marc.* 14).

Whereas Celsus had presented what might be called a "social" argument against Christians, Porphyry offered a historical argument. How could Christ, who had appeared only lately, be the savior of all humankind? "Let them not say that the human race was saved by the ancient Jewish law, since the Jewish law appeared and flourished in a small part of Syria, a long time after [the ancient cults in Italy], and only later made its way into the Italian land, after the reign of Gaius Caesar, or probably during his reign. What, then, became of the souls of Romans or Latins who were deprived of the grace of Christ which had not yet come until the time of the Caesars?" (in Aug. *ep.* 102.8). How could the new way inaugurated by Jesus be truly universal?

Although Porphyry's writings against the Christians were answered by a series of Christian thinkers in the fourth century, his work was still being read at the end of the century. When Augustine set out to write the *City of God* in the fifth century, Porphyry was very much on his mind, and his defense of traditional piety set the agenda for one of the most important discussions of religion in Christian antiquity (*City of God,* book 10).

As we know from the famous passage in book 7 of the *Confessions,* Augustine was helped on his journey to Christianity by reading the *libri Platonici,* which meant the writings of Porphyry and Plotinus. The Platonists taught that humans cannot attain blessedness except by participation in the light that is something other than oneself; this is the God "on which all depends and to which all look and in which all are and live and think, the cause of life and mind and being." Hence Augustine can say that "in spite of your irregular terminology you Platonists have some kind of an intuition of the goal to which we must strive, however dimly seen through the obscurities of a subtle imagination" (*civ. dei* 10.29).[13]

Augustine believed that Porphyry had a glimpse of the "country in which we must find our home," yet because he only "saw it from afar off and with clouded vision," he had lost his way in trying to reach it. He had seen the goal of the quest, the one true God, but was distracted by inferior practices and lesser gods; for example, he had defended the traditional sacrifices of the Greek cities. How could he, a reasonable man, asks Augustine, think that animal sacrifices are necessary to God or that they are of any use to him? The sacrifice that God desires, says Augustine, is "an act that is designed to unite us to God in a holy fellowship," and this can only be the sacrifice of ourselves, not the offering of an external thing.

The words of Psalm 73 stand at the center of Augustine's theology, *"mihi adhaerere Deo bonum est"* ("to cleave to God is good"), and the theology of the early church. Human beings can only find fulfillment and peace in fellowship with God. Though Augustine and Origen disagreed on many theological points, on

13. Augustine's way of formulating the difference between himself and Porphyry is noteworthy. He is critical of his "irregular terminology" *(verba),* i.e., the names he uses for God (*civ. dei* 10.29).

this matter they are one.[14] Religion was not simply a matter of experience, or an imaginative response to the mystery at the core of things, or the uplifting pursuit of virtue, or the cement that binds together the social world; it is an affair of affection and love of a God who could be named and identified, whose ways were known, and with whom one could have genuine fellowship.[15] The authentic vision of God, the vision that nurtures "true religion," is a "vision of such beauty," says Augustine, and "altogether deserving of such a love," that a person who "fails of it is altogether unfortunate no matter how richly endowed one may be with any other kind of goods" (*civ. dei* 10.6).

Conclusion

All the ancient critics of Christianity were united in affirming that there is *no one* way to the divine. On its face this appears to be a positive theological argument. Indeed Porphyry's book *Philosophy from Oracles* is a collection of "oracles" of the peoples of the ancient world for the purpose of setting forth the traditional religious beliefs which had guided and enlightened people over the centuries. Yet it is clear that his work was directed chiefly at Christianity.[16] Likewise

14. Origen writes: "From a desire to implant in us the blessedness which comes to us as a result of knowing him, God is concerned to enable us to obtain friendship with Him through Christ and the constant indwelling of the Word" (*Cels.* 3.6).

15. Celsus had argued that the seers of old have helped human beings to gain "some conception of the nameless [God]." Origen responds that this was not enough because people still continued to worship things that were not God. When the "divine Logos, who was in the beginning with God, became flesh," God showed "more regard for the needs of mankind." Then Origen adds: "But we affirm that human nature is not sufficient in any way to seek for God and to find Him in His pure nature, unless it is helped by the God who is the object of the search" (7.42).

16. See Robert L. Wilken, "Pagan Criticism of Christianity: Greek Religion

Symmachus's *Relatio,* Julian's *Against the Galilaeans,* and Celsus' *True Doctrine,* though written in defense of the traditional religious practices, were inspired by the claims of the new religion.[17]

It was not the kaleidoscope of religious practices and feelings that was the occasion for the discussion of religious pluralism in ancient Rome; it was the success of Christianity, as well as its assertions about Christ and about Israel. To be sure, in antiquity there was a debate about the relativity of moral principles (is justice a matter of convention or nature?) prior to the advent of Christianity, but the religious form of the question was prompted by the spread of Christianity. To put the matter somewhat differently, the appeal to religious pluralism was a response to biblical religion, and hence to a history which had begun with Abraham (*Cels.* 6.4; *civ. dei* 10.32). Christianity of course is not unique in this regard; it shares the burden of this history with the Jews and, not insignificantly, with the Muslims. On this point, the defense of Abrahamic religion, Christianity must learn to make common cause with Muslims as it has with Jews.

By appealing to a particular history as the source of knowledge of God, Christian thinkers transgressed the conventions that governed civilized theological discourse in antiquity. Celsus asked with astonishment: "What is the purpose of such a descent on the part of God?" To which Christians answered: human beings are not capable of finding God by their own intellect and imagination; God had to come to them.[18] The starting point of Chris-

---

and Christian Faith," in *Early Christian Literature and the Classical Intellectual Tradition,* ed. W. R. Schoedel and R. L. Wilken (Paris, 1979), 117-134.

17. Celsus had read Justin Martyr's apology, and his book was inspired by Justin's work. See Carl Andresen, *Logos and Nomos. Die Polemik des Kelsos wider das Christentum* (Berlin, 1955).

18. "He who came down to human kind was originally 'in the form of God' [and] because of his love for human beings 'emptied himself' that all *might be able to receive him*" (*Cels.* 4.15).

tian theology must always be, in the words of 1 John, "what we have heard, what we have seen with our eyes, what we have looked at and touched with our hands, concerning the word of life . . ." (1 John 1:1).

Many of the issues discussed in the early Christian apologies — for example, fate and free choice, providence, origin of evil, the nature of God — had long been the subject of philosophical debate. On many points Christian thinkers reasoned no differently than their pagan counterparts, citing the same texts, presenting the same arguments, drawing the same conclusions. Even in discussions of the nature of God, they followed the teachings of the philosophers — for example, that God was uncreated, eternal, invisible, impassible, incomprehensible.[19] Nevertheless they asserted, against the philosophers, that the appearance of God in history had revealed the true God with a clarity and brilliance that had not been evident earlier (*Cels.* 7.42).[20] As much as Origen and Augustine were convinced that Christianity offered the only certain way to fellowship with God, in assessing the religious practices of the Roman world they did not simply assert the superiority of Christianity over the traditional rites. Rather they argued that the way proclaimed by Christ is to be preferred, *because* it sets the mind and heart on the proper object of love and devotion. That is why Christian thinkers, unlike Porphyry, could not view other religious practices with equanimity. Not every path to the divine is sound or elevating. Just because rituals are awesome, or observed by people for

19. On this point see *Cels.* 7.42, where Celsus says that knowledge of God comes either from "synthesis," i.e., from successive abstractions, by analysis (gradually moving from visible things to invisible realities), and by analogy. A similar idea is present in the Middle Platonists, for example, Albinus, *epit.* 10.5-6.

20. See also *Cels.* 4.14: "Not even [the philosophers] have been able to perceive clearly the true conception of God's nature, as being entirely incorruptible, simple, uncompounded, and indivisible."

generations, or defended by sophisticated thinkers does not mean that they promote fellowship with God.[21]

What is most noteworthy about the early apologists is that their criticism of the ancient religious practices was concrete and specific; they made judgments of what they observed in the cities of the Roman Empire. And they concluded that the beliefs that undergirded them were unworthy of God. For this reason they sought to persuade others that they could love God more ardently and cleave to God more fervently if they sought God alone, without the mediation of lesser gods, and without the succor of rites which do not purify the soul. In this they were correct, and their judgments have stood the test of time.

For Christians there can be no "theology of religions," only a theology of particular religions. What Christians have to say to Jews is different from what they said to the adherents of Mithra or Isis, just as what they say to Muslims is different from what they say to Buddhists. That what is said to one tradition differs from what is said to another implies that what one learns from one tradition differs from what one learns from another. Christian theology is not a closed system; it is able to recognize and respect elements of truth in other religions and to integrate these truths into itself. The particular claims of Christian faith are not, as often supposed, the end of dialogue, but its beginning. For if Christians cannot speak with others about what they know, there will be no conversation.

The debate over religious pluralism, however, was not simply a matter of theological ideas. From its inception it had a social and ecclesiological dimension. Christians had constituted a new

21. John Hick says that the "Copernican revolution in theology . . . involves a shift from the dogma that Christianity is at the centre to the realization that it is God who is at the centre . . ." (*God and the Universe of Faiths* [New York, 1973], 131). The difficulty with this position is that it cannot discriminate between religions, and assumes, without argument, that all religions equally serve God.

kind of community, one that was independent of the social and political institutions of the Roman Empire; it was not territorial, that is, defined by people or region or city, and its central rite, the *Sacrifice,* as it was called in Christian antiquity, embraced old and young, male and female, slave and free, gentile and Jew, rich and poor, educated and uneducated. Such a community was without precedent, and it figured large in the theological response to pagan criticism of Christianity.

Within Christianity the reality of God is never confined to the Logos. As Rowan Williams writes: "The doctrines of Christian credal orthodoxy are not, as is regularly supposed, insuperable obstacles to dialogue; the Incarnation of the Logos is not the ultimate assertion of privilege and exclusivity, but the center of that network of relations (implicit and explicit) in which a new humanity is to be created."[22] For Origen the church inaugurates this new possibility. In it he had found a community of people who "offer true worship to God" (7.7). For him the church was not an exclusive club, but a fellowship which by making "those outside of it . . . familiar with [its] sacred words and acts of worship" leads them to fellowship with the God of all.

That such a community existed in Origen's time and exists today there can be no doubt. Indeed, just as Moses was a more successful teacher of humankind than Plato, one might say that Jesus has proven to be a nobler teacher than Porphyry. For whatever its failings and shortcomings, the church has these many centuries offered true worship and praise to God, and that for Christian thought is a datum of considerable import.

22. Rowan Williams, "Trinity and Pluralism," in Gavin D'Costa, *Christian Uniqueness Reconsidered: The Myth of a Pluralistic Theology of Religions* (New York, 1990), 11.

3

No Other Gods

ONE OF THE LESSONS read at the Easter vigil is the story of Shadrach, Meshach, and Abednego in the fiery furnace. It is a good story, told well and not without irony. Each year when it is read I can hardly conceal a smile as the author lists (and not just once) the titles of the king's advisors — the satraps, prefects, governors, counselors, treasurers, justices, magistrates, and officials of the provinces — or as he takes delight (again not just once) in naming the musical instruments that called people to worship the golden statue — the sound of the horn, pipe, lyre, trigon, harp, drum, and the entire musical ensemble. This year, however, it was another section of the lesson that caught my attention. After the deliverance of Shadrach, Meshach, and Abednego from the fiery furnace, King Nebuchadnezzar says, "Blessed be the God of Shadrach, Meshach, and Abednego. . . . They disobeyed the king's command and yielded up their bodies rather than serve and worship any god except their own God" (Dan. 3:28).

Originally published in *First Things*, November 1993, pp. 13-18. Reprinted with permission.

It is a sign of the times that on the holiest night of the year the phrase from Daniel, "serve and worship any god except their own God," leaped out at me. In the past I remember listening intently as Genesis 1, the account of the Passover, or the exhortations of Deuteronomy were read to the newly baptized. But this Easter the words of King Nebuchadnezzar brought to mind the First Commandment: You shall have no other gods besides me. In the waning years of the twentieth century the time has come for Christians to bear witness to the worship of the one true God.

Practical atheism, that is to say, secularism, has undermined beliefs, attitudes, and conventions that have nurtured our civilization for centuries. The changes we are witnessing are not the inevitable alterations by which older ways adapt to new circumstances. They are the result of a systematic dismembering, a "trashing" of our culture that is "intentional, not accidental," as Myron Magnet puts it in his recent *The Dream and the Nightmare.* Nothing is left untouched, whether it be our most cherished institutions, or the roles that have defined one's place in family, neighborhood, and city, or assumptions about duty, love, virtue, honor, and modesty. All are subject to the scalpel of impatient and haughty reformers; what has been received from our parents and grandparents and from their parents and grandparents must submit to our unforgiving formulas for correction.

The goal, of course, is to dismantle the common Western culture, to turn everything into a subculture. Secularism wants religious practice, especially Christian practice, banished to a private world of feelings and attitudes, while at the same time the realm of the public is to be expanded to include every aspect of one's life. The earlier secularist appearance of tolerance toward religion is now seen to have been a sham.

Nor does secularism sustain any sense of obligation to the past. The texture of memory that is essential to a common culture cannot be sustained if the past is not lovingly transmitted to those who come after — even should some of its monuments offend us.

Christianity has proved to be more tolerant than the current revisionists. As the French philosopher Rémi Brague observed, Christian culture "resisted the temptation to absorb in itself what it had inherited from either the Greeks or the Jews — to suck in the content and to throw away the empty husk."[1] Over its long history the Christian tradition has cultivated a studied openness to the wisdom of former ages, even when such wisdom provided intellectual resources with which to challenge Christian faith. Think how the *philosophes* in their attacks on Christianity depended upon their legacy from antiquity. Yet for centuries, Christian institutions have nurtured the study of the classics. Christianity is an essential ingredient in our culture, says Brague, for its form "enables it to remain open to whatever can come from the outside and enrich the hoard of its experiences with the human and divine."

The ferocity of the current assault on the legacy of Christian culture, however, has brought a new clarity of vision. The alternatives are set before us with unusual starkness: either there will be a genuine renewal of Christian culture — there is no serious alternative — or we will be enveloped by the darkness of paganism in which the worship of the true God is abandoned and forgotten. The sources of the cultural crisis, it turns out, are theological.

In his lectures on *Christianity and Culture*, T. S. Eliot posed the issue of the relation between Christianity and Western culture in terms that were remarkably prescient. Writing in 1939 on the eve of the Second World War, Eliot said that the "choice before

1. Rémi Brague, "Christ, Culture and the New Europe," *First Things,* Aug./Sept. 1992, pp. 36-40.

us is between the formation of a new Christian culture, and the acceptance of a pagan one." Distinguishing three epochs in the history of Christianity and Western culture, he spoke of the period when Christianity was a "minority in a society of positive pagan traditions," a second period when the society as a whole — law, education, literature, art, as well as religion — was formed by Christianity, and a third, our own period, in which the culture has become "mainly negative, but which, so far as it is positive, is still Christian." In his view, "a society has not ceased to be Christian until it has become something else." Yet, he continued, "I do not think that [a culture] can remain negative," and it is conceivable that there will be an attempt to build a new culture on wholly different "spiritual" foundations. Eliot's proposal is that the way to meet this challenge is to form a "new Christian culture."

His lectures are filled with much wisdom: for example, that "Christianity is communal before being individual," and that there can be no Christian society where there is no respect for the religious life. "I cannot," he says, "conceive a Christian society without religious orders, even purely contemplative orders, even enclosed orders." If we are to speak of a Christian society, we "must treat Christianity with a great deal more intellectual respect than is our wont. . . ." And we must be concerned to make clear "its difference from the kind of society in which we are now living." Above all there is his observation that touches more directly on theology: it is, he writes, a "very dangerous inversion" for Christian thinkers "to advocate Christianity, not because it is true, but because it might be beneficial." Instead of showing that "Christianity provides a foundation for morality," one must show "the necessity of Christian morality from the truth of Christianity." "It is not enthusiasm, but dogma, that differentiates a Christian from a pagan society."

Dogma and *truth* are not the kind of words that will pass the test of political correctness; yet — or perhaps therefore — they are most useful in helping us to identify precisely the distinctively theological task that lies before us. It is time to return to first principles, to the First Commandment, and to take up anew the challenge faced by Christians many centuries ago when the Christian movement was first making its way in the Roman Empire. Christians are now called to persuade others (including many within the churches) that our first duty as human beings is to honor and venerate the one true God, and that without the worship of God, society disintegrates into an amoral aggregate of competing, self-centered interests destructive of the commonweal. To meet that challenge, Christians must learn again to speak forthrightly about who we are and what we know of God.

The Christian faith, as Eliot reminds us, is concerned not simply with values or attitudes or feelings or even "beliefs" as we use the word today, but with truth. Christianity is based not simply on experience, tradition, inherited wisdom, and reason, but on God's self-disclosure in history. To be sure, Christian truth has been handed on through a learned tradition in which it has been formulated, criticized, analyzed, refined, and tested by experience. Thus it has been the bearer of wisdom about what is good in human life, about sexuality, about being young and growing old, about work and money, children and family, duty and sacrifice, about friendship and love, art, literature, and music. But, as Origen of Alexandria said in the third century in his response to charges brought against Christianity by its critics, the Christian religion has its origin in "God's manifestation not in human sagacity," in the appearance of the divine Logos in human form. Christian faith is grounded in what was made known in Christ and confirmed by the Spirit's witness in the church. Consequently, Christian thinking, whether about God, about Christ, about the moral life, or about culture, must always begin with what has been made known.

A pernicious feature of Christian discourse in our day is its tentativeness, the corrosive assumption that everything we teach and practice is to be subject to correction by appeals to putative evidence, whether from science, history, or the religious experience of others. Nicholas Wolterstorff and Alvin Plantinga call this the evidentialist fallacy, the claim that it is not rational for a person to be a Christian unless he "holds his religious convictions on the basis of other beliefs of his which give to those convictions adequate evidential support." In this view, one's religious beliefs are to be held "probable" until evidence is deployed from elsewhere to support and legitimate them. The "presumption of atheism" must be the starting point of all our thinking, even about God.

One way of responding to this line of thought has been to offer arguments for the existence of God based on what is considered evidence acceptable to any reasonable person. Conventional wisdom has had it that proof of the existence of God has to be established without reference to the specifics of Christianity (or Judaism) or to the experience of the church. Atheism is to be countered by a defense of theism, not of Christian revelation. But this strategy has failed. In his book *At the Origins of Modern Atheism*, Michael Buckley helps us to understand why. To defend the existence of God, Christian thinkers in early modern times excluded all appeals to Christian behavior or practices, the very things that give Christianity its power and have been its most compelling testimony to the reality of God. Arguments against atheism inevitably took the form of arguments from nature or design, that is, philosophical arguments without reference to Christ, to the sacraments, to the practice of prayer, to the church. Buckley's book is an account of how this came to be, but within its historical description is to be found an argument that the "God defined in religion cannot be affirmed or supported adequately . . . without the unique reality that is religion." Or, to put the matter more concretely: "What God is, and even that God is, has its primordial evidence in the person and in the event that is Jesus Christ."

What has given Christianity its strength as a religion, as a way of life, and as an intellectual tradition is that it has always been confident of what it knows and has insisted from the very beginning, again to cite Origen, that the "gospel has a proof which is peculiar to itself." This phrase occurs at the very beginning of Origen's defense of Christianity to its cultural despisers, his *Contra Celsum*. Celsus, a Greek philosopher who lived in the second century, had said that the "teaching" that was the source of Christianity was "originally barbarian," which meant that Christianity had its origins in Judaism. Origen grants the point and even compliments Celsus that he does not reproach the gospel because it arose among non-Greeks. Yet Celsus adds a condition. He is willing to accept what Christians have received from barbarians as long as Christians are willing to subject their teaching to "Greek proof," that is, to measure it by Celsus' standards as to what is reasonable. Celsus believes that "the Greeks are better able to judge the value of what the barbarians have discovered, and to establish the doctrines and put them into practice by virtue." This is presumptuous, says Origen, for it implies that the "truth of Christianity" is to be decided by a criterion external to itself; but, he continues, the "gospel has a *proof* which is *peculiar to itself* and which is more divine than a Greek proof based on dialectical arguments." This more "divine demonstration" St. Paul (1 Cor. 2:4) calls "demonstration of the Spirit and of power."

Insisting that the gospel has a "proof peculiar to itself" did not mean that Christian thinking ignored the claims of reason, dismissing questions that arose from history or experience or logic. In discussions with Greeks, Christian thinkers presented the new faith not only by reference to the Scriptures but also by appeal to classical literature and general conceptions, "common ideas" that they shared with other educated men and women.

Critics tried to brand the Christians as mere "fideists," but the charge rang hollow. From the beginning, Christians heeded the claims of reason, and it did not take long for their adversaries to learn that they were able to match them argument for argument. Pagan thinkers had no franchise on rationality. The existence of a serious dialogue between Christians and Greek and Roman philosophers, conducted at the highest intellectual level for over three centuries (the mid-second century to the mid-fifth), is evidence that Christian thinkers did not supplant reason by faith and authority. The assertion that the gospel had a "proof peculiar to itself" was not a confession of unreasoning faith but an argument that commended itself to thoughtful men and women.

At issue in the argument about reason was the question of its starting point. Origen argued that with the coming of Christ reason had to attend to something new in human experience. In the earliest period of the church's history Christian thinkers did not become philosophers in order to engage the philosophers. Or, to put the matter more accurately, to engage in philosophical discussion they did not assume a traditional philosophical starting point. In the philosophical texts of the time, knowledge of God was derived through certain well-defined ways of knowing: by a process of successive abstractions — for example, in the way one moves from a surface to a line and finally to a point in geometry; by analogy — that is, by comparing the light of the sun and visible things with the light of God and intellectual things; or by contemplating physical objects and gradually moving to the contemplation of intellectual matters. Against the intellectualism of these ways of knowing God, Christian thinkers argued that the knowledge of God rested on "divine action" and on "God's appearance" among human beings in the person of Christ. Even when speaking to the outsider, they insisted that it was more reasonable to begin with the history of Jesus (and of Israel) than with abstract reasoning. Reason could no longer be exercised independently of what had taken place in history and what had come to be because of that history: the new reality of the church, a people devoted to the worship of the one true God.

How this conviction worked itself out in Christian thinking can be seen in the work of one writer after another, in Athanasius' response to the Arians, or Augustine's efforts to disentangle himself from the sophistries of the Manichees. But for our purposes here, Origen is the most illuminating because he stands at the beginning of the Christian intellectual tradition. He was the first truly deep thinker to give a firm epistemological foundation to the claim that Christians had come to know the true God in the person of Christ.

One of the most familiar citations of Plato in this period was a passage from the *Timaeus* in which Plato wrote, "It is difficult to discover the Father and Maker of this universe; and having found Him, it is impossible to declare Him to all." This text was understood to mean that God was beyond our comprehension, though by the activity of enlightened minds it was possible to have some knowledge of God. Celsus had cited this passage in his argument against the Christians. Origen, in responding to Celsus, said that while Plato's statement was "noble and impressive," it rested on philosophical agnosticism. The best evidence of its limitation was that on the basis of such knowledge of God the philosophers had changed neither their lives nor their manner of worship. Even while claiming to know the true God, they went on worshipping the many gods of Greece and Rome — and went on defending such piety as well. For Origen, as well as for Augustine and other critics of the religion of the philosophers, this is the central point. Because their knowledge of God was limited to what they could know by the activity of the mind, they never came to a genuine knowledge of God. They kept falling back into idolatry. Had Plato known the true God, writes Origen, he "would not have reverenced anything else and called it God and worshipped it, either abandoning the true God or combining with the majesty of God things which ought not to be associated with Him."

The philosophers would not acknowledge that by "becoming flesh" the divine Logos made it possible for human beings to know God more fully than they could by means of human reasoning alone. "We affirm," writes Origen, "that human nature is not sufficient in any way to seek for God and to find Him in his pure nature, unless it is helped by the God who is the object of the search." The knowledge of God is unlike other forms of knowledge. For it begins with God, not with human reasoning, and how we conceive of God is dependent on the nature of the reality that is presented to us — in the language of the Bible, that which is *seen*. The Church Fathers relied heavily on the Gospel of John in their "epistemology," and especially on John's conjunction between "seeing" and "knowing." One of the most frequently cited texts is John 1:18: "No one has ever *seen* God; the only Son, who is in the bosom of the Father, he has made him *known*."

One sign of the impoverishment of Christian speech in our day is that the term "faith" has been emptied of its cognitive dimension. As the Swiss Catholic theologian Hans Urs von Balthasar recognized, the logic of Christian discourse has collapsed at this point. "Nothing expresses more unequivocally the profound failure of [theologies that separate the Christ of faith and the Jesus of history] than their deeply anguished, joyless, and cheerless tone: torn between knowing and believing, they are no longer able to *see* anything, nor can they be convincing in any visible way." He cites the now-classic essay of the French Jesuit Pierre Rousselot, "The Eyes of Faith," published in 1910. The word "eyes," says von Balthasar, "indicates that there is something there for faith to see and, indeed, that Christian faith essentially consists in an ability to see what God chooses to show and which cannot be seen without faith."

The key point here is that faith is not a form of interpretation, one perspective among others, but a seeing of what there is to see, and hence a form of knowing. Recall the opening words of the First Epistle of John: "We declare to you what was from the beginning, what we have heard, what we have seen with our eyes, what we have looked at and touched with our hands, concerning the word of life — this life was revealed, and we have seen it and testify to it, and declare to you the eternal life that was with the Father and was revealed to us. . . ." First John states the primal truth that Christian faith rests on witness to what has happened in history, hence the honored place of the *martyrs* (witnesses) in Christian memory. Yet the witness to what was "seen" is never a testimony simply of what has happened in the past. In his Commentary on 1 John, St. Augustine noted a curious feature of its opening words. John does not simply say that he is bearing witness to what he has seen and touched; he says that he is also bearing witness to the "Word of Life." It does not escape Augustine that the phrase "Word of Life" does not refer to the body of Christ which could be seen and handled. "The life itself has been manifested in flesh — that what can be seen by the heart alone might be seen also by the eyes for the healing of hearts. Only by the heart is the Word seen; flesh is seen by the bodily eyes. We had the means of seeing the flesh, but not of seeing the Word: the Word was made flesh which we could see, that the heart, by which we should see the Word, might be healed."

The testimony that the church bears from one generation to another is at once a seeing of what was seen and a seeing of what cannot be seen. It is a seeing of what was seen in that the testimony is about something that happened in space and time, something that could be seen with the eyes and touched with the hands, and which is part of events that preceded and followed; it is also a seeing of what cannot be seen, in John's terms, a "knowing," in that God who cannot be seen is revealed in the events. The testimony that 1 John brings is not simply a witness

57

to a historical event, as one might, for example, tell others about a parade that passed in front of one's house. For that which one "saw" was the "Word of Life," not simply the words and actions of Jesus of Nazareth.

Faith is not something that is added to knowing: it is a constitutive part of the act of knowing God. Origen grasped this point with characteristic profundity. In his commentary on John 2:22 — "After he was raised from the dead, his disciples remembered that he had said this; and they *believed* in the scripture and the word that Jesus had spoken" — Origen cites the words spoken to Thomas in chapter 20: "Blessed are those who have not seen and yet have come to believe." Then he asks: how could it be that those who have not seen and have believed are more blessed than those who have seen and believed? If that is the case, those who come after the apostles will be more blessed than the apostles. Origen's answer is that in this life faith is imperfect; only at the time of the Resurrection will it be complete. But faith will still be *necessary*. Without faith there is no knowledge of God. Hence it is possible to say of faith what Paul says of knowledge, "Now we believe in part." When the "perfection of faith comes," that which is partial will disappear, "for faith complemented by vision is far superior to faith through a mirror."

Faith's certainty comes from participating in the reality that is believed — that is, through fellowship with God. "By faith," writes Augustine, "we see and we know. For if faith does not yet see, why are we called *illuminati?*" It is not possible to know God from a distance, to be a spectator. Commenting on John 8:19 — "You know neither me nor my Father. If you knew me, you would know my Father also" — Origen explains how the term "know" is used in John and in the Bible as a whole. "One should take note," he says, "that the Scripture says that those who are united to something or participate in something are said to *know* that to which they are united or in which they participate. Before such union and fellowship, even if they understand the reasons given for something, they do not know it." As illustration he mentions the union between Adam and Eve which the Bible described as "Adam knew his wife Eve," and in 1 Corinthians 6:16-17, the union with a prostitute. This shows, he says, that "knowing" means "being joined to" or "united with." The knowledge of God, then, is experiential. No doubt this is one reason why the knowledge of God is always conjoined with the love of God in early Christian literature. Love implies familiarity, intimacy, union.

In terms such as these, early Christian thinkers defended the worship of the one God. The boldness of the intellectuals as well as the courage of the martyrs (in some cases, e.g., Justin Martyr or Origen, they were the same persons) rested on the certainty that comes from "seeing." In a sermon on Acts 1, John Chrysostom said, referring to the phrase "witness of the Resurrection," that the apostles, who were witnesses of the Resurrection, did not say, "Angels said this to me, but we have *seen* it." That is the inescapable foundation of Christian belief in God.

Matthew Arnold once said: "The uppermost idea with Hellenism is to see things as they really are." That puts things succinctly — and backwards. Early Christian thinkers insisted that the Greeks did *not* see things as they are. They only saw what lay on the surface. Like the pathetic creatures in Plato's cave, they saw only shadows and images. For this reason, it was the Greeks who had to be corrected, not the Christians. And on this basis Christian thinkers mounted an offensive against the pretensions of their culture. By ignoring the true God, their contemporaries not only did not know whom to worship or how, they failed to see that everything else in society — morality, art, literature, politics — was skewed. Hence, the early Christians were unwilling to bend the knee when they heard the sound of the horn, pipe, lyre, trigon, harp, drum, and entire musical ensemble. Their task, however, unlike that of Shadrach, Meshach, and Abednego, was intellectual. They not only made confession, they set out to persuade others that they could love God more ardently and cleave to God more fervently if they sought God alone without the succor of rites that do not purify the soul. In doing so, they laid the foundations for a new kind of society, one in which serving God faithfully was the highest duty.

Of course, it was easy for Christians to criticize pagan religion, with its many gods, its veneration of objects of wood and stone and gold, its divining and use of auguries and portent, and most of all, its practice of animal sacrifice. Even pagan thinkers were critical of the practices that defined religious devotion in the cities. Before the rise of Christianity, there was a well-established tradition of criticism of religion in the ancient world. Philosophical religion, however, was another matter entirely, for many things the philosophers taught were compatible with Christian theology. Augustine, it will be remembered, was helped in his move to the Catholic faith by reading the *libri Platonici,* which meant of course the books of the neo-Platonists, Porphyry and Plotinus. Yet Christian thinkers, including Augustine, were no less critical of the theological ideas of the philosophers than they were of the religious practices of their fellow citizens.

Although the philosophers had an intuition of the true God, in the view of Christian thinkers they did not know how to serve God. In a mordant passage in the *City of God,* Augustine, chiding Porphyry for proclaiming his devotion to the God of the Hebrews while venerating lesser gods, cites the words from Exodus: "Anyone who sacrifices to other gods instead of to the Lord alone will be extirpated." Augustine's argument is that worship is to be offered only to God, for "God himself is the source of our bliss, . . . the goal of our striving."

It has sometimes been argued that in the *City of God,* his apology *contra paganos,* Augustine made place for a neutral secular

60

space that could accommodate paganism and promote a "coherence of wills" about things relevant to this mortal life. Here there could be a joining of hands of the city of God and the earthly city for the cultivation of the arts of civilization. But for Augustine, a neutral secular space could only be a society without God, subject to the *libido dominandi,* the lust for power. He was convinced that even in this fallen world there could be no genuine peace or justice unless a society were to honor the one supreme God. There can, he writes, be no association of men united by a common sense of right where there is no true justice, and there can be no justice where God is not honored. "When a man does not serve God, what amount of justice are we to suppose exists in his being?" Where a people has no regard for God, there can be no social bond, no common life, and no virtue. "Although the virtues are reckoned by some people to be genuine and honorable when they are related only to themselves and are sought for no other end, even then they are puffed up and proud, and so are to be accounted vices rather than virtues."

In the *City of God,* Augustine is an apologist neither for a secular public space nor for theism. His great book is a defense of the worship of the one true God, the God who was acknowledged in ancient Israel, revealed in Christ, and venerated in the church. Like other early Christian apologists, he realized that it was not enough to make vague appeals to transcendent reality, to the god of philosophers, to a deity that takes no particular form in human life. The god of theism has no life independent of the practice of religion, of those who know God in prayer and devotion, who belong to a community of memory, and are bound together in common service. Only people schooled in the religious life, people like Shadrach, Meshach, and Abednego, can tell the difference between serving the one God faithfully and bowing down to idols. For Augustine, defense of the worship of the true God inevitably required a defense of the church, the City of God as it exists in time.

Eliot's *Christianity and Culture* admonishes us to take up the challenge of conceiving anew a Christian society. By a Christian society, he did not mean one that was composed solely of Christians, but one in which human life is ordered to ends that are befitting the true God. "It would be a society in which the natural end of man — virtue and well-being in community — is acknowledged for all, and the supernatural end — beatitude — for those who have the eyes to see it." Only God can give ultimate purpose to our lives and direction to our society. The First Commandment is the theological basis for a just and humane society.

I am reminded of a story I heard years ago in Germany when Walter Ulbricht, the German Communist leader, was head of the German Democratic Republic. It was said that Ulbricht once had a conversation with Karl Barth about the new society that was being built in East Germany. Ulbricht boasted to Barth that the Communists would be teaching the Ten Commandments in the schools and that the precepts of the decalogue would provide the moral foundation for the new society. Barth listened politely and then said: "I have only one question, Herr Minister. Will you also be teaching the First Commandment?"

4

Not a Solitary God:
The Triune God of the Bible

HE MUSLIMS HAVE a very distinctive term to apply to the
Christians. They call them "associators." The word first
occurs in Christian literature in St. John of Damascus,
who was born a generation after the Muslim conquest of the
Middle East. His father was the chief representative of the Christians to the Caliph who resided in Damascus and John, who
spoke Arabic, had contact with Muslim thinkers. In his monumental work, *The Fount of Wisdom,* written when he was a monk
at the monastery of Mar Saba in Palestine, he includes a long
chapter on Islam, one of the first efforts of a Christian thinker
to respond to the challenge of the new religion that had arisen
in Arabia several generations earlier. "[The Muslims] call us Associators," he writes, "because, they say, we introduce beside God
an associate to Him by saying that Christ is the Son of God and
God."[1] John was not simply passing on something he had heard

1. John of Damascus, *The Fount of Wisdom,* PG 94.768.

This essay will appear in a revised form in the *Companion Encyclopedia of Theology,* forthcoming from Routledge Ltd. in 1995.

from Muslim critics in Damascus or Palestine. He had studied
the Quran and knew that the charge could be found in the sacred
book of the Muslims. In Surah 3, "The House of Imram," it
reads: "Say, 'People of the Book! Come now to a word common
between us and you, that we serve none but God, and that we
associate nothing with Him, and do not some of us take others
as Lords, apart from God'" (Quran 3.54).

In the same treatise John of Damascus alludes to an even more
explicit passage from the Quran dealing with the deficiencies of the
Christian doctrine of God. Muhammad, says John, said that there
is one God "who was neither begotten nor has he begotten." The
reference here is to Surah 112, which in its entirety reads: "In the
Name of God, the Merciful, the Compassionate. Say: 'He is God,
One God, the Everlasting Refuge, who has not begotten, and has
not been begotten, and no one is equal to Him.'" It is clear from
this Surah that Muhammad was familiar with the Christian doctrine of the Trinity; indeed the Quran gives an Arabic translation
of two of the technical terms used in trinitarian theology, begotten
and unbegotten, *gen[n]etos* and *agen[n]etos*.[2]

To many Christians, not only to Muslims and Jews, the
doctrine of the Trinity appears as a theological construct, useful
perhaps as a way of explaining the manifold ways God is known
to us, but not a necessary teaching of the Christian faith. In the
early nineteenth century when Friedrich Schleiermacher organized his dogmatics, *The Christian Faith,* he relegated the doctrine
of the Trinity to an appendix. He acknowledged that the doctrine

2. Jews, of course, have been critics of the Christian doctrine of the Trinity,
but with the rise of Kabbalism in the medieval period, some Jewish thinkers
recognized similarities between kabbalistic ideas of *sefirot* (spheres) within God and
Christian notions of the divine persons, and hence acknowledged the place of
interdivine relationships within God. As one medieval Jewish thinker remarked:
"The idolators [Christians] believe in the Trinity and the kabbalists believe in a
tenfold God" (David Novak, *Jewish Christian Dialogue: A Jewish Justification* [New
York, 1989], 48-50).

expressed a fundamental truth about the union of the divine and human, but considered it a means of defending something else, an effort at theological explanation of more fundamental truths, not a teaching in its own right. The doctrine of the Trinity, he wrote, is not "an immediate utterance concerning the Christian self-consciousness." In his view there are only two immediate utterances, that the being of God is present in Christ, and that the Divine unites itself with human nature in the Spirit who animates the Church. Neither of these affirmations requires that one posit a triune God.

Schleiermacher's approach to the problem was not new. Already in the early church some had taught that the various terms, Father, Son, and Holy Spirit, were simply names that Christians give to the ways we know and experience God's activity and presence, the modes by which God is known. In calling God "Father," "Son," and "Holy Spirit," it was argued, we are only speaking about how God manifests himself to us; we are not saying anything about the nature of God. This question raised centuries ago by Sabellius, and echoed by later critics of the doctrine of the Trinity during the church's history, can be stated as follows: If we take it as axiomatic that God is one, is there any reason, on the basis of the several ways God is known to us, to project the plurality of our experience of God into the life of God? Why should the manifestations of God be thought to designate distinctions within the Godhead?[3]

---

3. On the doctrine of the Trinity in the early church, see J. N. D. Kelly, *Early Christian Doctrines* (New York, 1958), 109-137, 223-279; Jaroslav Pelikan, *The Christian Tradition*, vol. 1 (Chicago, 1971), 172-225. For a systematic presentation of the classical texts, see Thomas C. Oden, *The Living God: Systematic Theology*, vol. 1 (San Francisco, 1987), 181-225. For contemporary discussions drawing on patristic sources, see Robert Jenson, *The Triune Identity* (Philadelphia, 1982), and Wolfhart Pannenberg, *Systematic Theology*, vol. 1 (Grand Rapids, 1991), 259-336. For a recent historical survey of fourth-century developments, see R. P. C. Hanson, *The Search for the Christian Doctrine of God* (Edinburgh, 1988).

The Divine Wisdom

The first Christians were Jews who recited the ancient words of the Shema in their daily prayers: "Hear, O Israel: The Lord our God is one Lord; and you shall love the Lord your God with all your soul, and with all your might" (Deut. 6:4).[4] Jesus quoted the words of the Shema in answer to the question, "Which commandment is the first of all?" and the earliest Christians affirmed their belief in the one God. "We have one God the Father from whom are all things" (1 Cor. 8:6). The first commandment, according to the Shepherd of Hermas, is, "Believe that God is one, who created and completed all things and made all that is from that which is not . . ." (*Shepherd of Hermas*, Mandatum 1.1). The first article of the creed is "we believe in one God."

Though the earliest Christians were in agreement with their fellow Jews in confessing one God, from the beginning Christianity set itself apart from Judaism by the veneration it gave to Christ. This is apparent in the exalted language used to describe Christ in the New Testament — son of God, image of the invisible God, the eternal word who is with God, the one in whom the "fullness of the Godhead dwells," "the express image of God's very being"; in hymns in honor of Christ, for example, "God highly exalted him and gave him the name that is above every name" (Phil. 2); in the baptismal formula which yoked Christ, a human being, with God the Creator of all things; and in the early Christian Eucharist where Christ was celebrated as alive and present in the breaking of bread. As early as the second decade of the second century an outside observer, Pliny, the Roman governor of Bithynia, reported that Christians were in the habit of meeting on a fixed day before it was light to "recite a hymn to Christ as to a *god*."[5]

4. The Shema, as a biblical confession, remained authoritative for Christians. See Gregory of Nyssa, *Tres dii* (*PG* 45, 1120d).
5. *Epistle* 96.

One of the ways to reconcile the apparent conflict between worshipping Christ as God and venerating the one God, that is, to offer a rational account of the shape of Christian language and practice, was to draw directly on the Greek philosophical tradition. Because of the influence of Christianity and Judaism on Western thought, we are inclined to think of the divine as a category that has only one member (the one supreme God), but in antiquity the divine was a broad and expansive category of existence which included many different members. Within this tradition the most obvious way to deal with the "divinity" of Christ and the Holy Spirit was to conceive of a hierarchy of divine beings. One could acknowledge the existence of the one high God, while also venerating lesser deities, who, though they did not rule over the whole universe as did the one high God, were nevertheless considered divine. "The person who worships several gods, because he worships one of those which belong to the great God, even by this very action does that which is loved by him," wrote Celsus, the second-century pagan philosopher.[6]

Influenced by this understanding of the divine, some early Christian apologists, living in the polytheistic world of ancient Rome, thought it a shrewd strategy to accentuate the pluralistic character of Christian conceptions of the divine. Athenagoras, an apologist born in Athens who wrote in the latter part of the second century, informs his critics, with barely concealed glee at his cleverness in trumping an adversary: "Who . . . would not be amazed if he heard that folks who are called atheists bring forth God the Father, God the Son, and the Holy Spirit. . . . Nor does our teaching concerning the Godhead stop there, but we also say that there is a host of angels and ministers whom God . . . set in their places. . . ."[7] How can we be called atheists, implies

6. Celsus in Origen's *Contra Celsum* 8.2.
7. Athenagoras, *Legatio* 10.5.

Athenagoras, when we confess not one God but three gods and many lesser divine beings who are associated with these three? In Greco-Roman society the pluralism of Christian theology was not an embarrassment; for some it was a valuable selling point of the new movement.

Other apologists used similar language. Justin Martyr, for example, said that Christians honor Jesus Christ as the "son of the true God himself, and hold him to be in the second rank and the prophetic spirit in the third rank."[8] Origen of Alexandria even went so far as to use the term "second God"[9] with reference to the Son. In a discussion with a Christian bishop from Arabia, he said, "We are not afraid to speak in one sense of two Gods, and in another sense of one God."[10] As a temporary solution these ideas about the plurality of gods helped early Christian thinkers to explain how Christ and the Holy Spirit could be divine while retaining the belief that God is one, but under closer examination such formulations proved unsatisfying and were eventually discarded because they seemed to make the Son and the Holy Spirit into "assistants" to God, not "associates." Plurality with respect to God, however, had impressed itself on Christian thinkers from the very beginning.

Nevertheless when some in the churches heard theologians talk about a second God or about different ranks of deity, they believed that something had gone awry. After all, in becoming Christians they had been delivered from the worship of many

8. Justin Martyr in 1 *Apol.* 13.
9. Origen, *Comm. in Joan.* 6.202.
10. Jean Scherer, *Entretien d'Origène avec Héraclide et les évêques, ses collègues sur le Père, le Fils, et l'âme* (Cairo, 1949), 123. Origen explains that it is necessary "to show in what sense they are two and in what sense the two are one God" (124). ET in *Alexandrian Christianity,* ed. and trans. J. E. L. Oulton and Henry Chadwick (Philadelphia, 1954), 438.

gods to serve the one true God. Wasn't this talk of several gods a reversion to the life they had left behind? At the beginning of the third century, Tertullian of Carthage in North Africa, the first Christian thinker to write in Latin, said that the rank and file among Christians (he called them the "simple folk") believed that in preaching "two or even three Gods" the church's belief in one God was compromised. "'We hold,' they say, 'to the monarchy,'" the one single God who rules all things.[11] Because they held to the belief that there was one sole ruler, such Christians were called "monarchians," that is, adherents of belief in the single *(monos)* rule *(arche)* of God.

As one examines the writings of the criticism of monarchianism by the church's leading thinkers, for example, Irenaeus, Tertullian, or Origen in the early period, it is evident that something deep within Christian tradition was propelling Christian thinkers to move beyond received conceptions of God's oneness and unity. One of the sources for this ferment was of course the Bible itself, not simply the New Testament, but also the Septuagint. Within some Jewish circles prior to the advent of Christianity, "wisdom" *(sophia)* was pictured not simply as a divine attribute displaying God's activity in the world, for example, in creation, but also as a "divine agent," carrying out God's purposes for humankind. In time "wisdom," though closely associated with God and identified with God, came to be conceived as having a kind of independent existence in the heavenly realm. An important text is Wisdom of Solomon 7: "For wisdom is more mobile than any motion; because of her pureness she pervades and penetrates all things. For she is a breath of the power of God, and a pure emanation of the glory of the Almighty; therefore nothing defiled gains entrance into her. For she is a reflection *(apaugasma)*

11. Tertullian, *Adversus Praxean* 3.

of eternal light, a spotless mirror of the working of God, and an image of his goodness" (7:24-26). In the Wisdom of Solomon wisdom is called "the fashioner of all things" (7:22), "an associate in [God's] works" (8:4), a member of God's heavenly council who exists from eternity (24:9).[12]

The New Testament identifies Christ with Wisdom: "Christ the power of God and the wisdom of God" (1 Cor. 1:24). Hence one of the tasks of early Christian thinkers was to draw out the implications of identifying Christ with the figure of Wisdom as a divine agent portrayed in books such as the Wisdom of Solomon and Proverbs. Of course, the New Testament had pointed the way. For example, the opening sentences of the book of Hebrews use an expression that echoes the book of Wisdom: Christ is the "reflection *(apaugasma)* of God's glory and the exact imprint of God's very being" (Heb. 1:3). In his treatise *On First Principles,* Origen calls attention to the correspondence between such texts in the New Testament and passages from the Septuagint (besides the Wisdom of Solomon, also Prov. 8:22-25) as well as other passages in the New Testament that speak of Christ as the image of God, for example, "image of the invisible God" in Colossians 1:15. From these texts, he concluded that the "wisdom of God has her subsistence nowhere else but in him who is the beginning of all things." Because Christ is the Wisdom of God, argues Origen, he is rightfully called God. He is also called the "only son" of God, the one whose origin is to be found in God. To say, then, that Christ is the "image of God" means that he shares God's nature in the way that a child shares the nature of his parents.

Origen realized that the term "wisdom" was normally used adjectivally as in the phrase "wise man"; that is, "wisdom" referred

12. See in this connection Larry W. Hurtado, *One God, One Lord: Early Christian Devotion and Ancient Jewish Monotheism* (Philadelphia, 1988), 41-44.

to a quality or attribute or characteristic of a person. In conventional usage wisdom did not designate something that acted as an agent or existed independently of something else. Applied to the doctrine of God, the question was whether Wisdom (i.e., Christ) was to be understood as having its own proper existence, or whether Wisdom was a way of talking about a mode of God's existence in relation to human beings. In technical theological language the question was whether the figure of Wisdom was to be "hypostasized," that is, understood as an independent entity, albeit within God — what later theology would call "person."

The presence of passages in the Septuagint that spoke of Wisdom as a divine agent, indeed as the preeminent divine agent, helped Christians understand the language of the New Testament and gave them an initial conceptual framework to express, on the one hand, the belief that Christ is God, and on the other, that he is not simply a divine attribute or emanation but had his own proper existence. Wisdom, however, was only one "title" for Christ in the New Testament, and only as it was interpreted in light of other biblical titles, notably "son of God" and "Word *(logos)* of God," were Christian thinkers able to do justice to the reality that they had come to know in Christ. In his Commentary on the Gospel of John, Origen discussed these and other titles at length, for example, "light," "door," "way," "shepherd," "king," and "life"; but it was these three, "wisdom," "son," and "word," that were most important in formulating the church's doctrine of the Trinity.

Already in Origen's day the meaning of the term "logos" had become a matter of dispute within the Christian community. The question was asked whether "word" was to be taken in its conventional sense to mean something which has no existence apart from the one who speaks the word, or whether when used of Christ it had a different sense. The term "logos" occurs in the LXX version of Psalm 45:2 (44:2), which reads: "My heart uttered a good word." The "word" mentioned here and the "word" in the prologue to the Gospel of St. John were taken to be the same, and some Christians thought the meaning of the term was plain. "Word" was to be taken in its usual sense, hence it designated "an utterance occurring in syllables," that is, a sound that disappears as soon as it is heard. Applied to Christ, this meant that he had no existence apart from the Father.[13]

Origen admits that it is difficult to understand how one can speak of a "word" in the same way that one can speak of a "son." Hence the term "word" should be interpreted in conjunction with the title "son," a term that implies "having life in itself." Though a son receives life from his mother, he exists as a human being independent of her. If the terms "word" and "son" are taken together it is clear that "the word is distinct from God (the Father) and has its own existence." Origen reminds his reader that in reading the Bible one must discern the *sense* of the terms used: when one reads the term "door" or "vine" or "way" no one thinks that Christ is an actual door or a vine or a path. These terms must be taken as intended, that is, to refer to something spiritual that is *like* a door or a vine.[14] The Word of God, then, must be understood as something that is *like* a human word, but is not a human word. The "word of God," writes Origen, has its own "individuality, i.e. has life in itself," and in this way is to be distinguished from word or reason in human beings, "which has no individuality apart from us."[15] The Scriptures teach, says Origen, that the "Son is other than the Father," that is, has his own proper existence.[16]

Tertullian had come to a similar conclusion though his reasoning is somewhat different. Like Origen he argued that the titles in the Scriptures should not be taken in isolation; no one

13. *Comm. in Joan.* 1.151.
14. *Comm. in Joan.* 1.152-157.
15. *Comm. in Joan.* 2.191.
16. *Comm. in Joan.* 10.246.

title could be taken as definitive in and of itself, not Word, not Son, not Wisdom. The Scriptures speak of the same "power . . . now with the name of wisdom, now with the designation word." The several titles complement each other. Hence in answer to those who took Psalm 45 ("My heart has uttered a good word") to imply no distinction between God and his "word," Tertullian cites other texts applied to Christ that speak of Christ as the "son." If one argues that the word spoken by the Father cannot be distinguished from the Father, it would seem that the son in Psalm 2:7, "You are my son, this day have I begotten you," must be the same as the father, which is absurd.[17]

Equally significant is Tertullian's analysis of the term "word" or "reason," *logos* in Greek, *ratio* in Latin. He argues that there is a sense in which reason in human beings, and hence in God, can be understood to have its own existence. Consider, says Tertullian, that as a human being made in the image and likeness of God "you have reason within yourself. . . . Consider how when you deliberate silently within yourself by reason, this same action takes place within you [that takes place in God]; reason accompanied by discourse *(sermo)* meets you at every moment of your thought, at every impression of your consciousness; your every thought is discourse, your every consciousness is reason; you must perforce speak it in your mind, and while you speak it you experience as a partner in conversation *(conlocutorem)* that discourse which has in it this very reason by which you speak when you think in company of that [discourse] in speaking by means of which you think."[18]

Tertullian is making a simple but profound point. As human beings we think of ourselves as a single person, with our own individual consciousness, and we look at the world from the

17. *Adversus Praxean* 7 and 11.
18. *Adversus Praxean* 5.

perspective of our unique and distinctive "ego." Yet it is the universal experience of human beings, because they are rational creatures, that they have within themselves the power of reasoning. Reasoning is always dialectical, that is, it involves questioning, saying yes and then saying no, a back and forth in the mind as words, ideas, and concepts challenge, criticize, or confirm each other. This silent dialogue takes place within the mind without speaking a word. In thinking one becomes aware of an other within oneself which, paradoxically, is oneself. This other, of course, takes many different forms depending on the topic and the purpose of our deliberations, whether we are thinking alone or in discussion with someone else. Yet the other is always present in the form of a question, an alternative, a doubt, a contrary proposal, or a complementary thought. The very term "deliberation" suggests that thinking is a form of debate that goes on inside the self.

Because of the dialectical character of human reasoning, it is plausible, argues Tertullian, to speak of a kind of second "person" within us. "So in a sort of way you have in you a second discourse by means of which you speak by thinking and by means of which you think by speaking: discourse itself is another [than you]." Tertullian is not interested in establishing a truth about human psychology (though he wrote a large book dealing with the human soul) but in drawing an analogy between the human mind and the nature of God as God. Human beings were made in the "image and likeness of God." If it is the case that one can speak of a "partner in conversation" in the human mind, an "associate" if you will, "how much more completely . . . does this action take place in God, whose image and similitude you are authoritatively declared to be, that even while silent he has in himself reason, and in [that] reason discourse." Therefore it is not unreasonable to say that God is not a solitary monad. "So I have been able without rashness to conclude that even then, before the establishment of the universe, God was *not alone,* seeing he continually had in himself Reason, and in Reason Discourse, which he made another beside himself by activity within himself."[19]

The Resurrection of Christ and Christian Reasoning

The interpretation of the biblical titles of Wisdom, Word, and Son took place in conjunction with the account of Christ's life as recorded in the Gospels. The New Testament presents Christ as a human being born of a woman, who lived the life of a child, grew to maturity, taught and worked miracles in the villages and towns of Galilee, was crucified in Jerusalem, executed on a cross, and three days after his death raised to new life. This portrait was indelibly part of Christian thought and experience. Hence when Christians used phrases such as the "Wisdom of God" or "Word of God," or said that in Christ "the fullness of God dwelled bodily," they had reference to a concrete historical person as well as a divine being who existed in intimate fellowship with God. What they knew of God's Wisdom or Word was disclosed to them not only through the Scriptures but also by the life of Christ, that is, by what had happened in history. The several titles were complementary and had to be interpreted in relation to one another. God's Wisdom may have been known through reading the Septuagint, but the Son could not be clearly discerned in the Septuagint without first knowing the Son who lived on this earth.[20] As St. Irenaeus put it at the end of the second century: "According to the economy of our redemption there are both father and son."[21]

19. *Adversus Praxean* 5.

20. The term "son" occurs in Ps. 2:7, "You are my son, today I have begotten you"; this psalm was interpreted christologically in the early church.

21. *Demonstration* 47. The importance of the "economy" is echoed in the

Irenaeus uses the term "economy," an expression that is puzzling to modern readers but essential for understanding the Christian doctrine of the Trinity. In Christian theology the term "economy" designates God's ordered self-disclosure in creation, in the history of Israel, and preeminently in the life, death, and resurrection of Christ.[22] Hence the term was used as a shorthand way of referring to the Incarnation and the events that had followed from God's descent into human affairs, that is, to the evangelical history. More than any other term it captured what was unique to Christianity, and that was, in the words of Ignatius of Antioch early in the second century, the suffering and death of Christ: "Now the Gospel has something distinctive; the coming of the Savior, our Lord Jesus Christ, his suffering and resurrection."[23]

Tertullian's chief argument against the "monarchians" is that in claiming to safeguard belief in the one God, they ignore the economy, that is, the evangelical history. They do not understand that "while they must believe in one God only, yet they must believe in him *along with his economy*."[24] In his view, and in the view of all early Christian thinkers, thinking about God has to begin with history, specifically the appearance of God in the person of Christ. Reasoning about God had to proceed differently now than it had before the coming of Christ. The rank and file, whom Tertullian condescendingly calls the *simpliciores,* fail to see this and "take fright at the economy."

---

liturgy, for example, in the Eucharistic prayer in the Apostolic tradition which says that in taking on flesh within the womb of the Virgin the Word was "*manifested as God's son*" (Hippolytus, *The Apostolic Tradition,* chap. 4).

22. In the Wisdom of Solomon, "Wisdom" is closely identified with the major events in Israel's history, e.g., the creation of Adam; Abraham, Lot, and Sodom; Jacob and Joseph; the Exodus; the wanderings in the wilderness; and the conquest of the land (see chapters 10–12). On this point, see Hurtado, 43.

23. Ignatius, *Philadelphians* 9.2.

24. *Adversus Praxean* 3.

The difficulty with the "monarchians" was that they stead-fastly held to conceptions of God that were formed before the coming of Christ. Of course, it should be acknowledged that the critics of monarchianism also suffered from a kind of theo-logical inertia. On certain points, for example, notions of divine impassibility and immutability, they too clung to older concep-tions of the divine. Origen, for example, said that as a result of "God's descent to human affairs," that is, the economy, we "have been able to perceive clearly the true conception of God's na-ture." Yet when he states what has been learned he uses conven-tional Greek categories: God is "incorruptible, simple, uncom-pounded, and indivisible."[25] Tertullian, more than his contem-poraries, realized that the "economy" required a more radical critique of earlier philosophical notions of God.[26] But all agreed that thinking about God had to begin with the economy, God's ordered self-disclosure in history. "The human mind," writes Gregory of Nyssa, "can only speak about God as it is instructed by God's works," that is, what is disclosed in the historical revelation in Christ.[27] The economy is the engine that drives trinitarian thinking.

How important the "economy" was in forcing Christians to revise their ideas of God can be seen in a passage from the fourth-century Latin theologian, Hilary of Poitier, sometimes called the "Athanasius of the West" because he spent most of his life, which spanned the fourth century (he was born about 300 C.E. and died in 367), defending the decrees of the Council of Nicaea in 325 C.E. He was also a biblical interpreter from whom we have a commentary on the Gospel of Matthew and a com-

25. *Contra Celsum* 4.14.

26. Joseph Hallman, *The Descent of God: Divine Suffering in History and Theology* (Minneapolis, 1991), 51-77.

27. Gregory of Nyssa, *Contra Eunomium* 2.154, ed. Werner Jaeger, vol. 1 (Leiden, 1960), 270.

mentary on the Psalms (covering about fifty psalms). But his greatest achievement was a large work entitled *On the Trinity*, written at the height of the Arian controversy. In this work Hilary shows not only that he has mastered the arguments of earlier writers but also that he was able to rework them with great originality. It is from him that I took my title "Not a Solitary God." Hilary writes: "We cannot as true believers assert that God is one, if we mean by it that he is alone. . . ." If God were solitary and alone, that would give no place for his Word. If, on the other hand, we simply assert that the Son is a second God alongside of the supreme God, we deny that God is one. We must, says Hilary, confess: "Though he is one he is not solitary."[28]

That Hilary would frame the issue in this way is significant. The Arians had argued that the Son was not wholly divine. The Scriptures, for example, called him the "first born of all creation" (Col. 1:15), that is, he was "made," and other passages (e.g., Prov. 8:22) suggested that he should be ranked as the highest of created beings. In their response, the defenders of the Nicene formulas (e.g., "true God from true God . . . begotten not made, of one substance with the Father [*homoousion*]"), Athanasius and others, tried to show, by an exegesis of disputed texts from the Scriptures, that Christ was fully God.[29] The question raised by the Arians concerned the status of the Son, not the nature of God. Hilary of course joined other Nicene thinkers in defending the full divinity of the Son; but in the passage I have just cited he moves the debate into new territory by making it a discussion of the nature of God.

His argument runs as follows. The first Christians were Jews, and as Jews they recited each day the ancient prayer of the Jews, the

---

28. Hilary of Poitier, *De Trinitate* 7.3.
29. See for example Athanasius, *Orations Against the Arians* 1:37ff. and passim. Text in *PG* 26, ET in *N.P.N.F.*, Series 2, vol. 4.

Shema, "Hear, O Israel, the Lord your God is one." Since this is so, asks Hilary, what are we to make of Thomas' confession, "My Lord and my God"? How could Thomas have confessed Jesus, a human being, as "my God" and at the same time pray the Shema? How could a faithful Jew and apostle forget the divine command to recite the Shema and make a new confession, that Christ is God, when he knew that his very life depended on the confession that God is one? Thomas had often heard Jesus say things such as "I and the Father are one," and "all things that the Father has are mine," as we know from the Gospel of John.

What is striking about Hilary's argument is that it is so consciously historical. He explains that the facts of history, that is, the "economy," forced a rethinking of the traditional way of conceiving God. Hilary envisions a time at the very beginning of Christianity when all Christians were Jews and continued to observe Jewish traditions. His comments indicate that he had asked himself a question that I am sure many have asked, especially when reading St. Paul. How could a faithful Jew, formed by Jewish tradition and accustomed to Jewish rites and prayers, for whom the most fundamental article of faith was that God is one, how could Paul use such exalted language about Christ and employ on occasion formulas of greeting that link Christ with God, for example: "The grace of our Lord Jesus Christ, the love of God, and the fellowship of the Holy Spirit be with you all" (2 Cor. 13:13)?

Hilary's answer is that everything was transformed with the resurrection of Christ, and Thomas was the first to grasp the nature of the change. Once Jesus was raised, Thomas "understood the whole mystery of the faith through the power of the Resurrection." For "no nature is able to rise from death to life by its own power except God's nature. . . ."[30] *Now,* that is, in light of the resurrection, Thomas was able to confess Christ as God

---

30. Hilary, *De Trinitate* 7.12.

"without rupturing his loyalty to the one God," for he saw that his confession was not the "acknowledgement of a second God, nor a betrayal of the unity of the divine nature." The resurrection of Christ teaches us, says Hilary, that God is not a "lonely God" or an "isolated God" *(in solitudine),* yet at the same time it does not teach us that there are two Gods.[31]

For Hilary, the resurrection of Jesus was the basis for rejecting a strictly monistic view of God. One cannot exaggerate the significance of this reasoning for the development of the Christian doctrine of the Trinity. The economy not only reveals God's purposes for humankind; it also discloses the inner life of God. In the words of a contemporary theologian, Wolfhart Pannenberg: "As God reveals himself, so he is in his eternal deity."[32] Though God is ineffable and his ways beyond finding out, the Scriptures teach that in Christ we not only come to know the "face" of God but are able to look within God. A striking text in this regard is Colossians 1:19, "In [Christ] all the fullness of God was pleased to dwell." With characteristic boldness, Origen took this passage to mean that through God's revelation in Christ we become "spectators" of the "depth of God."[33]

Hilary, then, has reason to say that through Christ's resurrection the apostles learned something of God that was not evident prior to the "economy." He expresses what is implicit in early Christian discussions of the Trinity and states the reasoning that was at work in early Christian thinking about God. The event in Christ's life that was decisive in God's self-disclosure, the event that sealed and completed his mission, was the resurrection from the dead. Through the resurrection Christ's unique relation to God was made apparent. In the words of St. Paul, Christ "was

31. *De Trinitate* 6.19; 7.2.
32. Pannenberg, *Systematic Theology,* 1:300.
33. *Comm. in Joan.* 20.1.

declared to be Son of God with power according to the spirit of holiness by resurrection from the dead" (Rom. 1:3).

The Son Never Acts Alone

What had been disclosed in the economy gave early Christian thinkers the confidence to explore the nature of God afresh, guided of course by the Scriptures. Thinking about God could no longer be carried on independently of what had occurred in the evangelical history. In the strict sense of the term, the argument that God was not a "solitary God" was not concerned with the doctrine of the *Trinity*. The debate focused on the status of the Son and whether the Son or Word is an emanation from the Father or whether the Logos has its own proper identity.[34]

Christian language, however, is resolutely tripartite.[35] This is most evident in the formula used at baptism: "In the name of the Father and of the Son and of the Holy Spirit." But there were also such expressions within the Bible, for example, the greeting at the conclusion of 2 Corinthians, "The grace of our Lord Jesus Christ, the love of God, and the communion of the Holy Spirit be with you all," or the opening words of 1 Peter: "To the exiles . . . who have been chosen and destined by God the Father and sanctified by the Spirit to be obedient to Jesus Christ and to be sprinkled with his blood" (1 Pet. 1:2). Of these passages J. N. D. Kelly wrote in his book *Early Christian Creeds*:

34. As Origen put it at one point, the heretics either "deny that the individual nature of the Son is other than that of the Father" or they "deny the divinity of the Son and make his individual nature and essence as an individual to be different from the Father" (*Comm. in Joan.* 2.16).

35. There are, of course, bipartite formulas in the New Testament, e.g., 1 Cor. 8:6; 1 Tim. 2:5; Rom. 4:24. On this point see J. N. D. Kelly, *Early Christian Creeds* (New York, 1964), 19-23.

"In all of them there is no trace of fixity so far as their wording is concerned, and none of them constitutes a creed in any ordinary sense of the term. Nevertheless the Trinitarian ground-plan obtrudes itself obstinately throughout, and its presence is all the more striking because more often than not there is nothing in the context to necessitate it. The impression inevitably conveyed is that the conception of the threefold manifestation of the Godhead was embedded deeply in Christian thinking from the start. . . ."[36]

Although the church's language was "tripartite," it would take time for the doctrine of the Holy Spirit to be subjected to theological analysis. In the fifth century Augustine wrote: "There has not been as yet, on the part of learned and distinguished investigators of the Scriptures, a discussion [of the Holy Spirit] full enough or careful enough to make it possible for us to obtain an intelligent conception of what also constitutes his special individuality *(proprium)*. . . ."[37] By the end of the fourth century, as the teaching concerning the Son was being given its definitive form, the same thinkers who had written works dealing with the status of the Son began to address the topic of the Holy Spirit. Though their arguments deal with the distinctive work of the Holy Spirit, their reasoning is not dissimilar to that used to discuss the doctrine of the Son. That is, they argued for the divinity of the Holy Spirit from the economy — for example, the role of the Spirit in the work of Christ — as well as from the gifts of the Spirit to the church. History, as recorded in the Scriptures, and experience, especially liturgical experience, were seen as complementary, each serving to illuminate the other.

The reality of the Holy Spirit was evident in the church's life. In the central prayer in the Christian liturgy, the prayer said

36. Kelly, 23.
37. Augustine, *De fide et symbolo* 9.19.

over the bread and wine in the Eucharist (the anaphora), the bishop besought the Holy Spirit to descend on the gifts. In a third-century Roman example of the prayer, after reciting the narration of the institution of the Eucharist and bringing to memory the saving death and resurrection of Christ, the bishop would continue, "And we pray that you would send your Holy Spirit upon the offerings of your holy church; that gathering them into one, you would grant to all your saints who partake of them to be filled with the Holy Spirit. . . ."[38] Likewise when a new bishop was consecrated the other bishops laid hands on the candidate and prayed: "Pour forth now that power which is yours of your royal Spirit which you gave to your beloved servant Jesus Christ which he bestowed on his holy apostles. . . . And by the Spirit of high-priesthood give him authority to remit sins according to your commandments. . . ."[39] Catechumens were baptized in the name of the Father and of the Son and of the Holy Spirit, and trinitarian doxologies were sprinkled throughout Christian worship.

For the Christian doctrine of the Trinity these "experiences" were foundational. They were certain evidence that God's presence among his people was not restricted to the time of Christ's sojourn on earth. The Scriptures taught that after Christ's departure the Spirit would be sent on his followers: "When the Spirit of truth comes, he will guide you into all the truth . . ." (John 16:9; also 14:16 and 15:26). Beginning with the outpouring of the Holy Spirit on Pentecost and continued in the charisms in the life of the church, these promises had been confirmed. "Having received the promise of the Holy Spirit, he has poured out this that you both *see* [!] and hear" (Acts 2:33). Just as Christ had given evidence of who he was when he dwelled on earth, so

38. Hippolytus, *Apostolic Tradition* 4.
39. *Apostolic Tradition* 9.

the Spirit gave evidence of his presence in the sacraments, in the witness of the martyrs and the lives of holy men and women, in the succession of bishops since the apostles. Gregory of Nazianzus wrote: "The Spirit dwells among us, offering us a most clear display of himself."[40]

The opponents of the developing trinitarian theology, however, argued that the Nicene theologians "bring in a strange God [the Holy Spirit] of whom Scripture is silent."[41] Everyone knew, of course, that the Spirit was mentioned in the Scriptures, for example, in the baptismal formula in Matthew 28 or the triadic greeting at the end of 2 Corinthians. At issue was whether the redemption in Christ was accompanied and completed by the work of the Holy Spirit. In response to this challenge Christian thinkers pointed to those passages that link specific actions in Christ's life with the work of the Spirit. "Consider the following," writes Gregory of Nazianzus in his theological oration on the Holy Spirit: "Christ is born, the Spirit is his forerunner (Luke 1:35); Christ is baptized, the Spirit bears witness (Luke 3:21-22); Christ is tempted, the Spirit leads him up (Luke 4:2, 14); [Christ] works miracles, the Spirit accompanies him (Matt. 12:22, 28); Christ ascends, the Spirit takes his place (Acts 1:8-9)."[42] In the Scriptures Christ's works are not presented as activities of the Son alone. God's revelation in Christ is made possible through the presence of the Holy Spirit. The tripartite nature of God is evident in the way Father, Son, and Spirit relate to each other in the events of revelation. Gregory of Nyssa writes: "With regard to the divine nature . . . we do not *learn* [from the Scriptures]

40. Gregory of Nazianzus, *Oratio* 31.26.
41. Gregory of Nazianzus, *Oratio* 31.1.
42. *Oratio* 31.29. To round out his argument Gregory gives a list of titles taken from the Scriptures, a "swarm of testimonies" as he calls it, for the Holy Spirit that identify the Spirit in relation to God (the Father) and Christ: "the Spirit of God," "the Spirit of Christ," "the mind of Christ," "the Spirit of the Lord," and others.

that the Father does something on his own, in which the Son does not co-operate, or that the Son acts on his own without the Spirit. Rather every operation which extends from God to creation and is designated according to our different conceptions of it has its origin in the Father, proceeds through the Son, and reaches its completion by the Holy Spirit."[43]

It is sometimes said that the doctrine of the divinity of the Holy Spirit is a deduction based on the logic of Christian thinking about the status of the Son. There is some truth to this view, but it does not do justice to the explicit statements in the Scriptures about the work of the Spirit in the economy.[44] An example is the passage in Romans 8:11, "If the *Spirit* of *Him* who raised *Jesus* from the dead [note that Father, Son, and Spirit are involved in a single activity] dwells in you, he who raised Christ from the dead will give life to your mortal bodies also through his Spirit that dwells in you."[45] Athanasius of Alexandria cites this passage in his first *Letter to Serapion,* an important document from Christian antiquity expounding biblical texts on the Holy Spirit. In the same letter he also cites 1 John 4:12-13: "If we love one another, God lives in us, and his love is perfected in us. By this we know that we abide in him and he in us, because he has given us of his Spirit," glossing that verse with the words from the Gospel, "Those who love me will keep my word, and my Father will love them, and we will come to them and make our home with them" (John 14:23). From these and other passages

43. *Tres dii* (*PG* 45, 1120d); ET in *Christology of the Later Fathers,* ed. E. R. Hardy and C. C. Richardson (Philadelphia, 1954), 261-262.

44. See in this connection Theodoret Stylianopoulos, "The Biblical Background of the Article on the Holy Spirit in the Constantinopolitan Creed," *La signification et l'actualité du IIe Concile Oecumenique pour le Monde Chrétien d'aujourdhui* (Geneva, 1982), 155-173.

45. Also 2 Cor. 1:21-22: "But it is *God* who establishes us with you in *Christ* and has annointed us, by putting his seal on us and giving us his *Spirit* in our hearts as a first installment."

Athanasius concludes that through the gift of the Holy Spirit we share in God's life and become heirs of God with Christ. "The Spirit," writes Athanasius, "is no stranger to the Son."[46]

The Son always acts in conjunction with the Holy Spirit, never on his own. On that point the Scriptures are clear. To be sure, the Bible does not make explicit statements about the divine status of the Holy Spirit; but neither does it say explicitly that Christ is "God" without qualifier. In the Scriptures, however, the Spirit is called a gift of living water (John 7:39) that brings life to those who receive it. He is the one who "gives life" to our mortal bodies (Rom. 8:11). Unlike creatures who *receive* life from someone other than themselves, the Holy Spirit *bestows* life and sanctification. Commenting on the phrase in John 1:13, "begotten of God," Cyril of Alexandria wrote: "Those who have been reborn by the *Spirit* through faith are called and indeed are begotten *of God*." When the Spirit dwells in us we become "temples of God" (1 Cor. 3:16; 2 Cor. 6:16).[47] Only God could rise from death to life, and only God can bestow life.[48] Again and again Christian thinkers argue that in the Scriptures the activity of the Spirit is the work of God, a point echoed in our century by Karl Barth. "According to these statements [in the Scriptures] the work of the Holy Spirit in revelation is a work which can be ascribed only to God and which is thus expressly ascribed to God."[49]

The church fathers also observed that in some passages the biblical writers speak not only of the work of the Spirit in the economy, but also of the Spirit's life within God. An important text is 1 Corinthians 2:10: "The Spirit searches everything, even

46. Athanasius, *Epist. 1 ad Serap.* 20.
47. Cyril of Alexandria, *Comm. in Joan.* 1.13; 1.9 (ed. Pusey 1:136).
48. Athanasius, *Epist. 1 ad Serap.* 1.23.
49. Karl Barth, "The Doctrine of the Word of God," Prolegomena to *Church Dogmatics,* vol. 1, part 1 (Edinburgh, 1936), 467.

the depths of God. For what human being knows what is truly human except the human spirit that is within? So also no one truly comprehends what is truly God's except the Spirit of God." In his book on the Holy Spirit, written in the late fourth century, Basil interpreted this text (he cites it twice): "But the greatest proof that the Spirit is one with the Father and the Son is that He is said to have the same relationship to God as the spirit within us has to us."[50] As God is revealed, so is the internal life of God.

Biblical Language and Divine Kinship

The shape of the classical doctrine of the Trinity was given by the Holy Scriptures. The church fathers insisted that the Scriptures held a privileged place in Christian thinking. Consequently they were chary of efforts to "translate" its terms and concepts into a conceptual idiom that was thought to be more intelligible. To be sure some thinkers, for example Gregory of Nyssa, drew on philosophical terms and concepts to aid in expounding the Bible. Yet even Gregory believed that the biblical language was irreplaceable. This is apparent in a fascinating exchange between Gregory and a fellow bishop who was sharply critical of the creed adopted at Nicaea. The question had arisen whether the biblical terms "Father," "Son," "Holy Spirit" could be replaced by other terms that were more precise philosophically. In place of "Father,"

---

50. Basil, *De spiritu sancto* 40. John of Damascus cites 1 Cor. 2:11 at the beginning of *fid. orth.*: No one, he writes, knows the Father except the Son (Matt. 11:27) and the Holy Spirit "who knows the things of God as the spirit of man knows the things that are in him" (*fid. orth.* 1.1). Basil also cites Rom. 1:26, "the Spirit himself intercedes for us." Some said this indicated that the Spirit was inferior to the Father because an intercessor is always inferior to a benefactor. A few lines later Basil responds with the verse about the Son: "He is at the right hand of God, and intercedes for us" (Rom. 8:26, 34; *spir. sanct.* 50).

"Son," and "Holy Spirit," Eunomius had substituted what he considered more appropriate expressions: "the highest and most authentic being" to designate the Father; "the one who exists because of that being and after that being has supremacy over all the rest" for the Son; and a "third . . . subject to the one because of causation and to the other because of the activity by which it exists" for the Holy Spirit.

The difficulty with Eunomius' proposal, says Gregory, is that in the name of philosophical precision, he ignores the scriptural names of Father, Son, and Holy Spirit, which have been used by Christians in all parts of the world since they were first handed on by the apostles. It is neither "pious nor safe to alter the text of the creed [or the Bible] in this new direction," says Gregory.[51]

Now one might reply that Gregory, by appealing to the authority of Scripture and tradition, ignores the real issue: How is the language of the Scriptures to be adapted, and perhaps reformulated, so that it becomes intelligible to people who have been formed in a Hellenistic culture? Eunomius' translation of the scriptural language was based on a judgment as to what was philosophically intelligible within Greco-Roman culture. The language of the Bible, as interpreted by Christian tradition, cut against the grain of what were considered well-grounded conceptions of the nature of divinity.

Gregory was of course as much aware of the philosophical difficulties of traditional conceptions of the divine as was Eunomius. Yet he defends the scriptural language and offers arguments as to why it should be preserved, and further, why it is to be preferred over the terms proposed by Eunomius. The words one uses, argues Gregory, cannot be indiscriminately exchanged, as though what they designate will remain the same no matter what the vehicle. Words carry connotations and associations; they

51. *Contra Eunomium* 1.158 (ed. Jaeger 1:74).

are not simply referential. They bear dimensions of meaning that would be lost if they were replaced by other terms. This is particularly true of metaphorical words such as "Father" and "Son." The term "Father," for example, is quite different from "supreme and absolute being," and "Son" from "one existing after the other," because when the words "Father" and "Son" are spoken, the listener recognizes at once "the proper and natural relationship to one another" that the terms imply. These terms signify a relationship that the others do not. By abandoning the terms "Father" and "Son" Eunomius does not simply jettison the biblical language; he also abandons "the idea of relationship which enters the ear with the words."

The point to be noted is that the terms "Father" and "Son," in contrast to words such as "Logos" or "Wisdom," are directly related to the revelation of God in Christ, that is, to the economy. The term "Father" is seldom used in the Old Testament to speak of God. It occurs in some key passages, for example, in the oracle to David, transmitted by the prophet Nathan, that God will establish an everlasting kingdom in which he will be a "Father" to the house of Israel (2 Sam. 7:14). It also occurs occasionally in the prophets. But it only appears eleven times in the Old Testament with respect to God, whereas in the New Testament Jesus invokes God as "Father" over 170 times. The New Testament intensifies the identification of God as Father.[52] Gregory realized that the terms "Father" and "Son," which came into general use among Christians because of God's appearance in Christ, imply a "kinship" between Father and Son that is at the heart of trinitarian theology. By abandoning the terms "Father," "Son," and "Holy Spirit," Eunomius is forced to jettison the very thing that is most distinctive of God.

52. On this point see Janet Martin Soskice, "Can a Feminist Call God 'Father'?" in *Speaking the Christian God: The Holy Trinity and the Challenge of Feminism,* ed. Alvin F. Kimel, Jr. (Grand Rapids, 1992), 88.

The idea of kinship suggested that "relation" is a primary characteristic of the divine life. The term "Father," for example, does not designate God's "nature" but an internal relation within God. Likewise other terms that were used in trinitarian theology, for example, "unbegotten" *(agen[n]etos)* and "begotten" *(gen[n]etos),* were not abstract terms to speak of what is characteristic of divinity; "unbegotten" (the term used for God as the source of all things) is a relative term like the word "Father." It names the "relation in which the Father stands to the Son, and the Son to the Father," writes Gregory of Nazianzus.[53] The profound truth, learned from the economy, that the Son (or Wisdom or Word) was not simply an emanation from God but must be conceived as an "other" (a "co-speaker," or associate) gave "relation" a primary role in conceiving of God. As Robert Jenson writes: "The original point of trinitarian dialectics is to make the relations between the identities, . . . and therewith the temporal structures of evangelical history, constitutive in God."[54] God's work, as presented in the Scriptures, is never the activity of a solitary God.

How this truth, that relations among the "persons" of the Trinity were constitutive of God, was lived and experienced by Christians is most evident, as already noted, in the church's liturgy, preeminently in the anaphora, the great prayer said over the gifts of bread and wine and in the rite of baptism. But it also took root in Christian spirituality and speculative theology, as can be seen in a book written by Richard of St. Victor, a twelfth-century Latin theologian. If we agree, he says, that God is love, as we learn from the First Epistle of John, then we can say that this love is exhibited first and foremost in the love between the Father and the Son. Of course, some would say that the primary form

53. *Oratio* 29.16. "These names (Father and Son) make known a genuine and intimate relation. . . ."

54. Robert Jenson, *The Triune Identity* (Philadelphia, 1982), 119.

of love that is found in the Scriptures is the love God has "toward his own creation." But such love, responds Richard, can hardly be called "supreme love," for how could God love one supremely who is not deserving of supreme love?[55]

Richard is an earlier scholastic, and in the fashion of medieval theology, he presents his argument, not in the manner of the church fathers, that is, by citing Scriptural texts (except as a starting point), but by drawing inferences from what is already known. Hence he says: in order that "fulness of love might have a place within God" it was necessary that a divine person have a relation with an "equally worthy person," and such a person would, perforce, have to be divine. For just as love demands a plurality of persons, for one cannot love unless there is an other, someone to receive the love, so "supreme love demands equality of persons."[56]

By making love the central feature of the relation of the persons, and not the analogy of the mind, as had Augustine (who had explored the possibilities of a trinity of love in his *De Trinitate*), Richard was able to accent not only the plurality of persons but also the distinctive character of the relations within God. That is, he found a way that made "plurality" or "associates" within God philosophically compelling; in giving the Holy Spirit an equal place in the divine life, he helped make theology genuinely trinitarian, not simply binitarian, a theology of Father and Son.

In a remarkable passage that could only be written by someone who loved God but had also experienced human love, Richard wrote: "Where equal benevolence exists in either person it is necessary that each with equal desire and for a similar reason should seek out a sharer of his excellent joy. For when two persons

55. Richard of St. Victor, *De Trinitate* 3.2-3; ET by Grover Zinn, *Richard of St. Victor* (New York, 1979), 374-376.
56. Richard of St. Victor, *De Trinitate* 3.7.

who mutually love embrace each other with supreme longing and take supreme delight in each other's love, then the supreme joy of the first is in intimate love of the second, and conversely the excellent joy of the second is in love of the first." But then he adds: "As long as the first is loved by the second, he alone seems to possess the delights of his excellent sweetness. Similarly, as long as the second does not have someone who shares in love for a third, he lacks the sharing of excellent joy. In order that both may be able to share delights of that kind, it is necessary for them to have someone who shares in love for a third."[57] In Augustine, the Spirit is the love that binds the Father and the Son; in Richard, love is a third person without whom the love of the Father and the Son for each other is incomplete.[58]

The Muslim critics were correct. The Christians were associators. Because of the economy, they found it necessary to say that God the Father had asssociates. What is more, in response to the Muslims, Christian thinkers urged that such a way of conceiving God was preferable not simply because it was reasonable but because it was found in the biblical tradition that Muslims shared with Christians and Jews and was evident in the Quran. In discussion with Muslims, John of Damascus does not begin with arguments about the nature of God in general. The Quran, he notes, speaks of the "Word" and also of the "Spirit." In saying that the Word and the Spirit are "outside of God," and hence in "trying to avoid making associates of God," Muslim thinkers have "mutilated God." "It would be better to say that God has an associate than to mutilate God and deal with him as if he were a stone, or wood, or any of the inanimate objects. Therefore you accuse us falsely by calling us Associators; we, however, call you Mutilators of God."

57. Richard of St. Victor, *De Trinitate* 3.15.
58. See Augustine, *De Trinitate* 9.

Hilary's phrase "not a solitary God" was felicitous. In its original setting it was a tentative effort to find a way of explaining that after the coming of Christ it was not possible to conceive of God as a solitary monad. Though God was still confessed as one, God was not alone. But it led to more. If God is not solitary and exists always in relation, there can be no talk of God that does not involve love. Love unites Father, Son, and Holy Spirit, love brings God into relation with the world, and by love human beings cleave to God.

5

In novissimis diebus:
Biblical Promises, Jewish Hopes,
and Early Christian Exegesis

MICHAEL WYSCHOGROD, the Jewish philosopher, has observed that the State of Israel is a theological as well as a political problem for Christians. Some Christians, he wrote, find little difficulty in "validating the Jewish right to the land of Israel on the basis of biblical promises," but others (Wyschogrod has in mind the Holy See), by ignoring the biblical roots of the ancient promises of return to the land, "err in the other direction." Unless Christianity is to repudiate the ancient decision to "make the Hebrew Bible its own," it must realize that these promises are part of the scriptural tradition, and hence of concern not only to Jews, but "something the Church must struggle with." Nevertheless, many Christians, he writes, "persist in spiritualizing the promises of the land, an ancient strategy not easy to defend in the new theological climate of Jewish-Christian dialogue."[1]

1. Michael Wyschogrod, "The Bishops and the Middle East," *First Things*, April 1990, p. 16.

Originally published in *Journal of Early Christian Studies* 1 (1993): 1-19. Reprinted by permission of The Johns Hopkins University Press.

The "ancient strategy" of which Wyschogrod speaks is already evident in the New Testament, but it received its classical
expression in the commentaries on the Septuagint as well as in
exegetical and theological treatises written during the patristic
period. From the *Epistle of Barnabas* and Justin's *Dialogue with
Trypho* to the commentaries of Jerome and Cyril of Alexandria
and Theodoret of Cyrus on Isaiah or the Minor Prophets, one
can discern, in the midst of different social settings and among
a variety of exegetical techniques, wide agreement that the promises of the Jewish Scriptures are to be understood "spiritually."
Even Theodore of Mopsuestia, who was critical of the indiscrim-
inate application of prophetic texts to the life of Christ, recognized
that several psalms (2, 8, and 45) and some passages from the
prophets (e.g., Joel 2:28; Zech. 9:9; Mal. 4:5-6; and the book of
Jonah) referred to Christ.

Early Christian "spiritual" interpretation of the prophets has
of course been challenged by historical criticism. As A. Merx
observed over a hundred years ago in a study of the interpretation
of the prophet Joel in the early church: "Where allegory and its
deviations, anagogy and moral interpretation make their appearance, understanding of the text is destroyed."[2] As historical criticism has extended its hegemony over every aspect of scholarly
exegesis, similar views have achieved the status of an *opinio com-
munis.* What is noteworthy about Wyschogrod's objection to
patristic exegesis, however, is that it springs not so much from
historical-critical exegesis as it does from Jewish interpretation of
the prophets. Wyschogrod suggests, perhaps inadvertently, that
the exegesis of biblical promises about the land of Israel turns not
so much on a "historical" versus a "spiritual" interpretation of
the prophets but on how "later" events bear on the understanding
of the text. By posing the question in this way he helps us to

2. A. Merx, *Die Prophetie Joel und ihre Ausleger* (Halle, 1879), 112.

appreciate features of early Christian exegesis that have been ignored or forgotten.

Without appealing to the Hebrew prophets it would have been impossible for early Christian thinkers to formulate, much less defend, the claim that Jesus of Nazareth was the Messiah of the Jews. That is apparent in the early decades when most Christians were Jews and supported their conviction that Jesus of Nazareth was the promised Messiah by reference to the Septuagint. "All this took place to fulfil what the Lord had spoken by the prophet: 'Behold, a virgin shall conceive and bear a son, and his name shall be called Emmanuel'" (Matt. 1:22-23). But even when Christians moved into the larger society and addressed their message to Greeks and Romans, they appealed to the testimony of the prophets. In *1 Apology* Justin wrote: "There were among the Jews certain men who were prophets of God, through whom the prophetic Spirit announced in advance events that were to occur. . . . We find predicted in the books of the prophets that Jesus our Christ would come, born of a virgin . . . crucified, dying and rising again and ascending into heaven. . . ." (*1 apol.* 31).

From the beginning Jews challenged Christian interpretation of the prophets. The locus classicus is book 4 of Origen's *On First Principles,* where he discusses (according to Photius) "how the divine scriptures are to be read and interpreted" (*princ.* 4.1.1). The first topic Origen addresses is Jewish objections to Christian interpretation of the prophets. The Jews do not believe in "our savior," writes Origen, because "they think that one must follow the 'letter' when the prophets speak about him and because they are not able to see with their eyes that the things proclaimed about him have happened." As illustration of the Jewish argument Origen cites a number of passages from the prophets: Isaiah 61:1, "liberty to captives"; Ezekiel 48:15 and Psalm 46:4, the "building of a genuine city of God"; Zechariah 9:10, "cutting off the chariot from Ephraim and the war horse from Jerusalem," that is, the shattering of Israel's enemies; and Isaiah 11:6-7, "the wolf shall dwell with the lamb, and the leopard shall lie down with the kid. . . ."

In this debate the matter at issue is the character of the Messianic age, and hence of the community that will come into being at that time; for the prophets proclaim a future marked by untroubled joy and gladness, the end of war and strife, an age of peace and harmony among the nations of the world, of wealth and prosperity, a time when the people of God will serve God with their whole hearts and the Law will be observed perfectly.[3] Origen's Jewish critics make the reasonable argument that these things have not happened, hence the Messianic age has not yet arrived. Therefore Jesus cannot be the Messiah.

The Christian claim that Jesus is the Messiah was based on the correspondence between the historical events of Jesus' life and resurrection and a series of oracles from the Hebrew prophets.[4] Among the many texts that made up this building, the famous passage in Isaiah 2 was one of the cornerstones: "It shall come to pass in the latter days *(in novissimis diebus)* that the mountain of the house of the Lord shall be established as the highest of the mountains, and shall be raised above the hills; and all the nations shall flow to it, and many peoples shall come and say: 'Come, let us go up to the mountain of the Lord, to the house of the God of Jacob; that he may teach us his ways and that we may walk in

3. For a useful survey of Jewish Messianic expectations, see Emil Schuerer, *The History of the Jewish People in the Age of Jesus Christ,* ed. G. Vermes, F. Millar, M. Black (Edinburgh, 1979), 2:524-554.

4. There were other arguments: the events announced by the prophets had not happened in earlier Jewish history (Origen and Theodoret of Cyrus); the prophets would not have continued to repeat their oracles of restoration if the events they prophesied had come to pass. "If these things had happened to someone who lived long ago *(in veteribus),* those prophets who came later would not have prophesied that these things were going to happen in the latter days *(in novissimis temporibus)"* (Irenaeus, *Adv. Haer.* 4.34.3).

his paths.' For out of Zion shall go forth the law and the word of the Lord from Jerusalem" (Isa. 2:2-4; par. Mic. 4:1-3).[5]

This passage is not cited in the New Testament, but it is alluded to on several occasions, most notably in the opening words of the book of Hebrews: "In many and various ways God spoke of old to our fathers by the prophets; but in these last days he has spoken to us by a Son . . ." (Heb. 1:1).[6] The phrase "in the last days" is also cited in Acts 2 at the beginning of Peter's sermon on Pentecost. In this case it is the prophet Joel who is cited, but the text is conflated with the words of Isaiah 2. "In the last days it will be, God declares, that I will pour out my Spirit upon all flesh."

Just how important the phrase "in these last days" was to become can be illustrated by two well-known passages. It is quoted at the very beginning of Origen's *On First Principles.* The God of Adam, Abel, Noah, Abraham, Isaac, Jacob, Moses, and the prophets "in these last days, according to the previous announcements made through his prophets, sent the Lord Jesus Christ . . ." (*princ.* 1. pref. 4). And it occurs, significantly, in the decree of the Council of Chalcedon: "We confess one and the same our Lord Jesus Christ . . . begotten before ages of the Father in Godhead, the same *in the last days* for us. . . ." It is also cited early in Christian literature by Justin Martyr and Irenaeus and is used by Tertullian at key places in his *Adversus Iudaeos* and *Adversus Marcionem.*[7] So I need not belabor the point that "in these

5. For modern discussion of Isaiah 2 and Micah 4 and a survey of proposals concerning the literary relation between the two passages, see J. Vermeylen, *Du Prophète Isaïe à l'Apocalyptique. Isaïe I-XXXV* (Paris, 1977), 1:113-133.

6. See also Heb. 9:26; 1 Cor. 10:11.

7. Justin Martyr, *Dial.* 109; Tertullian, *Adv. Iud.* 3. Note that Tertullian says the prophecy refers to "us" who have been taught by the new law. Also in *Adv. Marc.* 3.21 where Tertullian discusses biblical promises concerning the land of Israel. For Origen, the phrase *"in novissimis diebus,"* cited in the first line of his *Homilies on Leviticus,* provided the hermeneutical key to his interpretation of the

last days" played a key hermeneutical role in early Christian thinking.

In this essay I am interested in tracing the phrase in commentaries on the book of Isaiah. For it is one thing to extract the phrase from the Scriptures and use it in a theological argument, something else to expound the text in a line by line biblical commentary. For in that genre historical and hermeneutical issues put a different kind of pressure on the interpreter. In a commentary, as Origen observed, it was not possible "to leave anything unexplained."[8] The length of his commentaries — thirty volumes on Isaiah, twenty-five on Ezekiel, thirty-two on the Gospel of John — gives a clue as to what he meant.

The first Christian commentary on the book of the prophet Isaiah was a massive work of Origen in thirty books. Unfortunately it is no longer extant.[9] Dionysius of Alexandria is reported to have written a commentary on Isaiah, but that too is lost.[10] The earliest extant commentary on Isaiah was written by Eusebius of Caesarea, who was a disciple of Origen and drew extensively on his commentary.[11] When Eusebius reaches chapter 2 in his commentary, he observes that this passage, which follows oracles critical of the

---

book (*Hom. in Lev.* 1.1). Jerome, in his letter to Dardanus (*Ep.* 129.8) on the meaning of the phrase "land of promise," alludes to 1 Cor. 10:11, *"in quos fines saeculi decurrerunt."*

8. Origen, *Hom. in Numeros* 14.1. For the difference between the scholia, homilies, and commentaries among Origen's exegetical works see E. Klostermann, "Formen des exegetischen Arbeiten des Origenes," *Theologische Literaturzeitung* 72 (1947): 203-208.

9. For discussion see Pierre Nautin, *Origène. Sa vie et son oeuvre* (Paris, 1977), 247-248. Nine homilies on Isaiah by Origen exist in a Latin translation prepared by Jerome (*PG* 13.219-254; critical ed. by W. A. Baehrens, GCS 33 [1925]).

10. See Jean Dumortier and A. Liefooghe, ed., *Jean Chrysostome. Commentaire sur Isaie,* SC 304 (Paris, 1983), 9-10.

11. Joseph Ziegler, ed., *Der Jesajakommentar,* in *Eusebius Werke* 9, GCS (Berlin, 1975).

"people of the circumcision,"[12] inaugurates a section on the calling of the gentiles. The prophet "gives a perspicacious sign of the time in which these things will take place."[13] It will be an age of peace when there will no longer be "toparchy and polyarchy, nations will not rise up against each other nor cities make war on each other. . . ." In Eusebius' view this can only mean the time of the Roman Empire after the coming of Christ. In this period the word of the Lord has gone forth from the "land of the Jews and from Zion itself" into all the world.[14]

Jews, however, apply the prophecy to the "people of the Jews" as though it referred to "their land."[15] They take the passage "in a bodily sense" to signify the "land of Palestine."[16] What Eusebius means by this term is that the Jews take the prophecy as a promise that will be fulfilled politically among the Jewish people, namely that the Jews would once again possess Jerusalem and Judea, the exiles will return, and a Jewish kingdom will be established in the land of Israel.[17] In Eusebius' day, Jews continued to anticipate the time when Jerusalem would again be the capital of a Jewish kingdom. In his discussion of Isaiah 5:1, "Let me sing for my beloved a love song concerning his vineyard . . . ," Eusebius remarks: "Some say that this passage refers to the land of Judea." They offer this interpretation because Judea is "fertile and fruitful," and they take the reference to a hill in the text to signify "the

---

12. Eusebius, *Comm. in Isaiam* (GCS, *Eusebius Werke* 9:14,16).

13. *Comm. in Isaiam* (GCS, *Eusebius Werke* 9:14,32–15,2).

14. *Comm. in Isaiam* (GCS, *Eusebius Werke* 9:15,13).

15. *Comm. in Isaiam* (GCS, *Eusebius Werke* 9:15,31-32).

16. *Comm. in Isaiam* (GCS, *Eusebius Werke* 9:16,12-13).

17. See also his commentary on Isaiah 4:2, "The fruit of the land shall be the pride and glory of the survivors of Israel" (Eusebius, *Comm. in Isaiam* [GCS, *Eusebius Werke* 9.26,36–27,5]).

royal metropolis that will be established in this same Jerusalem."[18]

For Eusebius the key to understanding Isaiah 2:1-4 is the phrase "in the last days," which is to be interpreted in light of passages from the New Testament that speak of the "end of the age," as for example Hebrews 9:26: Christ "appeared once for all at the *end of the age* to put away sin by the sacrifice of himself." The "last days" refers to the calling into being of a new community which is the offspring of the "Jerusalem above, the mother of us all."[19]

Two other commentaries from the fourth century, John Chrysostom's *Homilies on Isaiah* and the *Commentary on Isaiah 1–16* attributed to Basil of Caesarea, interpret Isaiah 2 along the lines set down by Eusebius. Each takes the phrase "last days" to be a key to understanding the passage and relate it to texts in the New Testament that speak of the "time" of Christ's coming. Pseudo-Basil alludes to Hebrews 9:26, which had been cited by Eusebius,[20] and John cites the phrase "fullness of time" in Galatians 4:4 and Ephesians 1:10.[21]

John was particularly conscious of the hermeneutical significance of the references to time in the book of Isaiah. He observed that chapter two begins with a superscript that suggests a kind of

---

18. Eusebius, *Comm. in Isaiam* (GCS, *Eusebius Werke* 9:9,14-17). The Jews, says Eusebius, understand the term "Judea" to mean "nothing more than the land of Palestine," and consider "earthly Jerusalem God's dwelling place": *Comm. in Psalmos* (*PG* 23.876d).

19. Eusebius, *Comm. in Isaiam* (GCS, *Eusebius Werke* 9:16,15-16. A similar argument appears at Isaiah 4:2: "The fruit of the land shall be the pride and glory of the survivors of Israel." This text, says Eusebius, speaks of the "entire earth and the whole world." The "survivors" who will be called "holy" (4.3) are those who are worthy to "be recorded for life eternal in the 'heavenly Jerusalem' (Heb 12.22)." *Comm. in Isaiam* (GCS, *Eusebius Werke* 9:26,36–27,5).

20. Ps.-Basil, *Comm. in Isaiam*, in *San Basilio. Commento al Profeta Isaia*, ed. Sac. Pietro Trevisan (Torino, 1939), 1:195-198.

21. John Chrysostom, *Hom. in Isaiam* (*PG* 56, 29a).

second beginning or at least a shift of subject matter from chapter one. Chapter one begins: "The vision of Isaiah son of Amoz which he saw against Judah and against Jerusalem in the days of Uzziah, Jothan, Ahaz, and Hezekiah, kings of Judah" (LXX). Chapter two begins: "The word that came to Isaiah son of Amoz concerning Judah and concerning Jerusalem" (LXX). Why, asks John, does the text repeat that Isaiah had a vision concerning Judah and Jerusalem? He replies that the book of Isaiah is composed of oracles that were pronounced "at different times," and that they were only later collected together in a book. In this respect the book of Isaiah differs from the letters of Paul or the Gospels, which were composed at one time. This means that different sections composed at different times often refer to different topics, and because these texts include prophetic oracles, to different times in the future. Chapter two then has a different "hypothesis," a different central theme than chapter one; indeed, it deals with "more sublime matters." Its subject is "the calling of the gentiles, the showing forth of the gospel, the knowledge of God extending throughout the whole world. . . ."[22]

With the meaning of "in these last days" clarified by reference to the New Testament, fourth-century Christian exegetes were able to give the details in the text a specifically Christian interpretation. Thus the phrase "all the nations" is taken to refer to the preaching of the gospel in all the world.[23] Similarly the phrase "on the highest mountain" was applied to the church, which is "visible to all human beings," not to the "temple of the Jews," which did not rest on the highest mountain. Mt. Zion was overshadowed by Mt. Olive, from which one looked down on the temple mount.[24] Further, the clause "out of Zion shall go

---

22. John Chrysostom, *Hom. in Isaiam* (PG 56, 27b).
23. Ps.-Basil, *Comm. in Isaiam* (Trevisan, 1:202-206).
24. John Chrysostom, *Hom. in Isaiam* (PG 56, 29b).

forth instruction" cannot apply to Moses for he received the Law not on Mt. Zion but on Sinai, and he did not himself enter into the land of promise. Hence Zion, which means Jerusalem, refers to the gospel, which began at Jerusalem and from there went into all the world.[25]

Now all this is familiar terrain and needs little elaboration. What I wish to note is that Eusebius, as well as other commentators on Isaiah, give their interpretation of this text a polemical cast and direct their observations against Jewish views of the text. Which is to say that the exegesis of the prophets did not take place in a vacuum; Christian interpreters had to defend their views in the face of rival claimants to the meaning of the text.[26] Hence the importance of the phrase "in the last days"; it gave a foothold for a Christian interpretation. In the words of the commentary of Pseudo-Basil, the passage is to be interpreted in light of the "great and exalted economy for the salvation of all human beings."[27]

Of course there are nuances of interpretation and different ways of rendering the specifics of the text, but Eusebius and John Chrysostom and Pseudo-Basil can be taken to reflect the central exegetical tradition up to the middle of the fourth century, which is to say before Theodore of Mopsuestia. For, as is well known, Theodore refused to give the text a messianic interpretation.[28]

Theodore was of course aware that this text had been inter-

---

25. Ps.-Basil, *Comm. in Isaiam* (Trevisan, 1:212); John Chrysostom, *Hom. in Isaiam* (*PG* 56, 32a).

26. On Eusebius' commentary and the Jews, see Michael Hollerich, "The Godly Polity in the Light of Prohecy: A Study of Eusebius of Caesarea's Commentary on Isaiah" (unpublished Ph.D. diss., University of Chicago, 1986).

27. Ps.-Basil, *Comm. in Isaiam* (Trevisan, 1:199).

28. Theodore's observations occur in his commentary on Micah 4, the parallel to Isaiah 2. See *Theodori Mopsuesteni Commentarius in XII Prophetas,* ed. Norbert Sprenger (Wiesbaden, 1977), 206-213. From Theodore we have no commentary on Isaiah.

preted christologically. He writes (in his commentary on Micah; the commentary on Isaiah is not extant): "I am amazed at those who say that these things spoken by the prophets about the Israelites when they were about to return from Babylon, are a kind of type that refers to what will happen at the time of the Lord Christ. Those who say that the return of the people from Babylon is signified by these things, I praise as speaking beautifully; but I do not know how one could be brought to say that this is a type of the events that took place at the time of the Lord Christ. For it is clear that every type has a correspondence to the thing of which it is a type."[29]

Theodore's principle is that the words of the prophets must be interpreted within the context of the time the prophet wrote unless there is "correspondence" between the text and the later events or the New Testament applies the text to later events.[30] In his view Micah 4 (and presumably Isaiah 2) fall in that category, even though certain passages in the New Testament use its language of "last days" to refer to the coming of Christ. Accordingly Micah is to be understood in the context of the events surrounding the captivity of the Israelites, first at the hands of the Assyrians, later by the Babylonians, and their hope of return and restoration. The text announces that there will be a "transformation of this place [Jerusalem] and the mount in which God commanded them to dwell will be stand out above all mountains. . . ." On that day the exiles will be gathered from many places as well as foreigners, God will be glorified in Jerusalem, and the Law will be observed. Theodore reasons as follows: "The phrase 'the law will go forth from Zion and the word of the Law from Jerusalem,' stands far from the dispensation at the time when Christ the Lord spoke

29. Theodore of Mopsuestia, *Comm. in Michaeam* (Sprenger, 206ff.)
30. Joel 2:28; Amos 9:11-12; Micah 5:1; Zech. 9:9; Mal. 3:1 (to John the Baptist); and the book of Jonah.

clearly to the Samaritan woman. 'Believe me woman, the time is coming, and now is, when the true worshipers will worship the Father in spirit and truth. . . .'" The words of Jesus show that when Christ comes God will not be worshipped in a particular place. In that day "preoccupation with places" will be eliminated and no preference will be shown to Jerusalem over other places. Micah, on the other hand, said that the Law will go forth "from Zion," and the word of the Lord "from Jerusalem." Hence the prophecy cannot be a type of Christ.

Theodore ignores the phrase "in the last days," the one feature of the text that other exegetes took to be the key to its interpretation. The only temporal reference that he discusses is the term "forever." Micah wrote: "And the Lord will reign over them in Mount Zion from this time forth and for evermore." Theodore realized that this phrase posed a problem for his reading of the passage, because no matter how one interpreted the prophecy, the deliverance of which it spoke had not lasted forever. After the return from exile Judea was a province of the Persian Empire, and later the city came under Ptolemaic and Seleucid rule. And of course Jerusalem was destroyed by the Romans in the first century of the common era, and in Theodore's day the Jews were still in exile. Furthermore Jerusalem was becoming a Christian city. Accordingly he interprets the phrase "forever" to mean "for a very long time."[31]

Why Theodore would depart from traditional exegesis of the prophets, even in cases where the New Testament guided that interpretation, has been a matter of continuing discussion among scholars. It is evident that the grammatical and literary techniques used to interpret classical authors influenced Theodore's exegesis of the Bible.[32] In this tradition the first question to be asked of

31. Theodore of Mopsuestia, *Comm. in Michaeam* (Sprenger, 209, 27).
32. Christoph Schaeublin, *Untersuchungen zu Methode und Herkunft der antiochenischen Exegese* (Koeln-Bonn, 1974).

any literary work concerned the purpose or *skopos* of the text as this was shaped by the historical setting, the author's intention, and the literary character of the work. But consideration of grammatical and literary questions was not unique to Theodore. Similar techniques were used by other writers, including Diodore of Tarsus, John Chrysostom, Jerome, Cyril of Alexandria, and Theodoret of Cyrus, to mention the more obvious exegetes from the fourth and fifth centuries.

Theodore has been singled out, however, because he applied the principles of grammatical and literary analysis more rigorously and seems to conform more closely to what contemporary scholars consider proper exegesis. A common observation about Theodore is that he practiced "sober, historical exegesis,"[33] the term "sober" serving as a kind of code word to set Theodore apart from other ancient commentators who practiced allegory or other forms of, shall we say, "inebriated" exegesis. Sprenger, in the introduction to his edition of the commentary on the Minor Prophets, praises Theodore for his criticism of "mythologizing" exegesis that "falsified the characteristic meaning of the Biblical text." In his view the presupposition for "good exegesis of the biblical text," that is, "historical-grammatical" exegesis, was knowledge of the historical circumstances.[34] Hence the Old Testament must be interpreted in its own setting, not in relation to the New Testament.

It is easy, especially in the twentieth century, when biblical scholarship has been dominated by the techniques of grammatical and historical criticism, to understand why Theodore has been lionized by scholars. He seems so much like ourselves. No less an exegete than Rudolf Bultmann wrote his second doctoral dissertation on Theodore of Mopsuestia, *Die Exegese des Theodor von*

---

33. Maurice Wiles in *The Cambridge History of the Bible,* ed. P. R. Ackroyd and C. F. Evans (Cambridge, 1970), 1:490.

34. Sprenger, *Theodori Mopsuesteni Commentarius,* 109.

Mopsuestia.[35] In this work Bultmann praised Theodore not only for his interest in the historical setting of the prophets, but also because he did not inject homiletical comments in his exegesis or use the text as a basis for dogmatic assertions.[36] Theodore possessed, it seems, that quality which is necessary for historical criticism: distance from the text. He realized that the text belonged to a different historical epoch (the Septuagint was an ancient book) and the task of the exegete was to interpret the text within its own original context. What had happened between the writing of the text and the interpreter was irrelevant to its interpretation. As Mariès put it early in this century in his study of Diodore of Tarsus, he brought to his task "the good sense of a reasonable man in the face of any text."[37] Before joining this chorus of praise for Theodore, it may be useful to look again at his exegesis in relation to *his* context and to the work of those he ridicules.

Theodore of course recognized that the Holy Scriptures are not only documents from the ancient Near East but also a book of the church. Certain passages of the prophets must be interpreted with reference to later events, more specifically with reference to the coming of Christ.[38] What he does not seem to take into consideration in his exegesis is that the words of prophets were a book of the

35. Rudolf Bultmann, *Die Exegese des Theodor von Mopsuestia,* ed. Helmut Feld and Karl Hermann Shelkle (Stuttgart, 1984). For Theodore, writes Bultmann, the text is not "Mittel zum Zweck, sondern Selbstzweck" (27).

36. When I read Bultmann's book on Theodore, I was reminded of Maurice Wiles' observation on Theodore: "Fourth-century Antioch was an outstanding centre of biblical scholarship and of ecclesiastical confusion. The former was not the primary cause of the latter, but the two were not wholly unconnected" (*Cambridge History of the Bible,* 1:489).

37. L. Mariès, *Études préliminaires à l'édition de Diodore de Tarse sur les Psaumes* (Paris, 1933), 129.

38. For example, Joel 2:28-32 (Theodore of Mopsuestia, *Comm. in Ioelem* [Sprenger, 95-98]). His principle seems to be that this and similar texts, e.g., Amos 9:11-12 (Theodore of Mopsuestia, *Comm. in Amos* [Sprenger, 155]) or Psalm 2, are given a christological interpretation in the New Testament.

synagogue as well as a book of the church. For the Jews the oracles of the promises were not moribund oracles about the distant past. They were also voices of hope and expectation. Which is to say that in antiquity there was a third claimant on the meaning of the Jewish Scriptures besides that of history and Christology, namely the hopes of the Jews.

To be sure, in disputes between Jews and Christians, Jews sometimes challenged Christian views by appealing to the historical setting in which the prophecies were written. For example, in the prologue to his *Commentary on Zachariah* Jerome said that he had "combined the historical views of the Hebrews with our spiritual exegesis."[39] And in his actual exegesis he often reports that Jewish interpreters refer the oracles of the prophets to the time of the captivity in Babylon or the period of return late in the sixth century B.C.E. Commenting on Ezekiel 28:25-26, "Thus says the Lord God: when I gather the house of Israel from the peoples among whom they are scattered . . . ," Jerome says that the Jews take this passage to be referring to the "time of Zerubbabel, Ezra and Nehemiah when the Jews returned from exile in Babylonia to dwell in the land of Judea."[40]

But the appeal to the original historical setting is only one side of Jewish exegesis of the prophets, and that the least important. Again Jerome is instructive. As often as he says that Jews interpret the prophetic oracles in the context of the exile and return from Babylon, he also reports that they refer the texts to the Messianic age which is yet to come. In his commentary on the passage from Ezekiel cited above Jerome goes on to say that other Jews believe Ezekiel is referring to something that has not yet happened and will be fulfilled "in the last time."[41] At Isaiah 58, "Your ancient ruins

39. Jerome, *Comm. in Zachariam-prol.* (*CChr* 76a, 748).
40. Jerome, *Comm. in Hiezechielem* 28.20-26 (*CChr* 75, 400).
41. Jerome, *Comm. in Hiezechielem* 28.20-26 (*CChr* 75, 400).

shall be rebuilt . . . ," the Jews "claim either that this took place under Zerubbabel and Ezra and Nehemiah *or* they refer it to the end of time, to the reconstruction of Jerusalem and the laying of deep foundations around the cities and the building of walls so high that no enemy can enter and all foes will be barred from them."[42] In short, the Jews, like the Christians, saw the oracles of the prophets as *promises,* hence like the Christians they were as much interested in their bearing on events that were subsequent to the prophets as they were in the original historical setting. Indeed, here is where the real dispute was to be found.

There seems to have been a genre of early Christian literature dealing with biblical promises, for example, Tertullian's lost work *De Spe Fidelium,* Dionysius of Alexandria's work *On Promises,* or book 2.11 of Origen's *On First Principles,* which is entitled "On Promises."[43] The works of Origen and Dionysius were directed against chiliastic interpretation of the biblical promises; Tertullian's work, however, was a defense of chiliasm along the lines set down by Irenaeus in the latter chapters of his *Adversus Haereses.*[44] In his *Commentary on Ezekiel* Jerome mentions Tertullian's *De Spe Fidelium* along with the writings of other chiliasts, Lactantius, Victorinus of Petau, Irenaeus, and Apolinaris.[45] In the same passage he also says that on the basis of this oracle Jews (and judaizing Christians) are hoping for the day "when the city of Jerusalem and the temple will be rebuilt."[46] Ezekiel is a book of promises that have not yet been fulfilled.

42. Jerome, *Comm. in Esaiam* 58.12 (*CChr* 73a, 672-673). On this topic see Robert L. Wilken, *The Land Called Holy: Palestine in Christian History and Thought* (New Haven, 1992), 133-137.

43. Tertullian, *Marc.* 3.24; Dionysius in Eusebius, *Hist. Eccl.* 3.24.

44. Irenaeus, *Adv. Haer.* 5.31-36.

45. Jerome, *Comm. in Hiezechielem* 36.1-15 (*CChr* 75, 500).

46. Jerome, *Comm. in Hiezechielem* 36.1-15 (*CChr* 75, 499).

The prophecy from Isaiah 2 was also such a promise.[47] According to the Jews, Isaiah spoke not only to his time, but also of a future that was yet to come. The evidence for this can be found in Jewish and Christian sources. In the second century Justin cited Micah 4:1-7 in his *Dialogue with Trypho*. He says to Trypho: "I am aware, that your teachers, sir, acknowledge that all the words of this passage were spoken of the Messiah."[48] Both Trypho and Justin agreed that the text was Messianic; the question was whether it had been fulfilled. For both Jews and Christians it was assumed that the meaning of Micah 4 is to be found not in the return from captivity in Babylonia but in the future Messianic age. Neither Jew nor Christian was interested in a strictly historical reading of the text.

Jews realized that the ancient prophecies to the Israelites during the Assyrian and Babylonian captivities had not come to perfect fulfillment during the period of the second temple. Jonathan Goldstein writes:

> Those unfulfilled prophecies each promised one or more of the following: the permanent liberation of the Jews from exile, from foreign rule, and from all mishap; the erection at Jerusalem of a temple more magnificent than Solomon's, which God Himself would choose as His own place, glorifying it and making it secure from desecration and destruction; the rule over the Jews of a great and just king from the dynasty of David; their exaltation to imperial primacy among the nations; the conversion of the gentiles to follow the ways of the true God; the coming of a permanent era of peace; the resurrection of the righteous dead; and the punishment of all the wicked, past and present.[49]

47. See Jerome's comments on the passage in Micah 4.
48. Justin Martyr, *Dial.* 110.
49. Jonathan Goldstein, "How the Authors of 1 and 2 Maccabees Treated the Messianic Promises," in *Judaism and Their Messiahs at the Turn of the Christian Era,* ed. J. Neusner, W. Green, and E. Frerichs (Cambridge, 1987), 69.

Though the temple had been rebuilt and some of the exiles had returned, the Jews remained subject to foreign powers. Hence they looked to a more complete restoration, in the words of Tobit, "when the times of the age are completed . . . just as the prophets said . . . (14:5).[50]

The hope of restoration was intensified after the destruction of Jerusalem by the Romans, and Isaiah 2 came to be one of the arsenal of texts from the prophets cited in support of the hope of rebuilding the temple. At the end of *Tractate Menacoth* (meal offerings) in the Tosefta, there is a discussion about the reasons why the several temples of the Jews were destroyed, the temple at Shiloh, Solomon's temple, and Herod's temple. Then the text asks: "What of the final building which is destined to be built — may it be in our lifetime and *in our days.*" In answer *Tractate Menacoth* cites Isaiah 2:2-3: "It shall come to pass in the latter days that the mountain of the house of the Lord shall be established as the highest of the mountains. . . ."[51] This tradition continued into the Middle Ages, as can be seen from David Kimhi's commentary on Isaiah. Commenting on Isaiah 2 he writes: "When the Scripture uses the phrase 'at the end of the ages' it refers to the days of the Messiah."[52] The Jews, it seems, were no more interested in the historical meaning of Isaiah 2 than

50. In the fragmentary *pesharim* on Isaiah found at Qumran the phrase "in the last days" refers to what is happening in the present and future. 4Q161 and 4Q163 in *Discoveries in the Judaean Desert or Jordan Qumran Cave 4,* ed. John M. Allegro and A. A. Anderson (Oxford, 1968), 13-14, 24.

51. T. Klauser writes: "When the Messianic expectations were not fulfilled in the time of Hezekiah, the nation — and perhaps also the prophet himself — postponed the fulfillment to a later time. Such postponement was natural and necessary. It was also proper. For the basic principle of the Messianic expectation is nothing else than the longing for the Golden Age in the future, whether near or distant. . . . And this basic principle is the secret of the eternal endurance of the Messianic expectations" (*The Messianic Idea in Israel* [New York, 1955], 57).

52. *The Commentary of David Kimhi on Isaiah,* ed. Louis Finkelstein (New York, 1966), 11.

were the Christians.[53] That Jews would sometimes urge a historical interpretation against the Christians was a polemical strategy
used to discredit Christian claims on the text.

Once the biblical prophecies are viewed in light of Jewish
hopes and are transplanted from the serene solitude of the scholar's study to the tumultuous arena of religious controversy, questions of interpretation take a quite different form. In that setting
the issue becomes: which events qualify as a likely fulfillment of
the text? To which future do they belong or to which community
are they to be applied? The Jews applied them to the future of
the Jewish people and the reestablishment of a Jewish kingdom
in the land. Christian commentators, in response, insisted that
they refer to the church. This is evident in a poignant and arrest-
ing passage in the *Dialogue with Trypho.* Justin had cited a number
of passages that refer to Israel, for example, "Israel my inheritance"
(Isa. 19:24) and "I will let men walk upon you, even my people
Israel . . ." (Ezek. 36:12). Trypho realized that Justin was claiming
that references to Israel in the prophets (and, one might add, in
the psalms and elsewhere) applied to Christians. Hence he asks:
"What is this? Are *you* Israel and is he speaking these things *about
you?*" Justin answers: "Yes."[54]

This exchange tells us as much about Jewish self-understand-
ing as it does about Christian exegesis. For Trypho the term "Israel,"
and its many biblical cognates, is univocal. It applied only to the

---

53. Isaiah 2 is cited, along with a series of other prophetic oracles, in an
apocalyptic poem written shortly after the Muslim conquest of Palestine. The poet
anticipates the day when the exiles would return and Jerusalem would be rebuilt as a
Jewish city. See Joseph Yahalon, "On the Value of Literary Works as Sources to
Elucidate Historical Questions," *Cathedra* 22 (1979): 133 (in Hebrew). The phrase
"in the last days" is cited in the apocalyptic work *Book of Zerubbabel,* which was written
(or re-edited) at the time of the Persian conquest of Jerusalem in the early seventh
century. The book's theme is: When will the time of deliverance come? See Even
Shmuel, *Midreshei Geuluh* (Jerusalem and Tel Aviv, 1954), 73, ln. 45.

54. Justin Martyr, *Dial.* 123. See also *Dial.* 11.

people who were descendants of Abraham. This was an acute problem for the early Christians. Is the new community born *within* Israel continuous with the Israel spoken of in the Scriptures, the "us" mentioned in Isaiah 2: "Let *us* go up to the mountain of the God of Jacob that he may teach *us* his ways and that *we* may walk in his paths"? Already in the song of Mary at the Annunciation, such an identification is made. "He has helped his servant *Israel,* in remembrance of his mercy, according to the promise he made to *our* ancestors, to Abraham and to his descendants forever" (Luke 1:55). But the point had to be reiterated as Christian thinkers sought to provide a credible interpretation of the Septuagint as a whole. In an offhand comment on the Annunciation to Mary, Eusebius of Caesarea grasped the essential point. The name Jacob or Israel "does not designate the Jewish people alone but all those from among all the nations who have been given the status of children of God when called by the Savior."[55]

With these considerations in mind, let us turn finally to the commentaries on Isaiah (and Micah) written in the fifth century by Jerome, Cyril of Alexandria, and Theodoret of Cyrus. For these expositors, though cognizant of Theodore's criticism, reaffirm that the key to understanding the text is not place, that is to say Mt. Zion, but time, the phrase "in these last days." And like earlier commentators their interpretation has a polemical edge. The Jews, says Jerome, take the "last days" to refer to the Messianic age, the "rule of the Messiah," which has not yet taken place and will occur at the "end of the ages."[56] At other places in his commentaries, in a similar context, he speaks of the Messianic age as the coming of "their Messiah," that is, the Messiah of the Jews, in contrast to the Christ of the Christians.[57]

---

55. Eusebius of Caesarea, *Comm. in Lucam* (*PG* 24, 532c). A similar identification is made in the song of Zechariah in Luke 1:68.

56. Jerome, *Comm. in Michaem* 4.1-7 (*CChr* 76, 472).

57. See Jerome, *Comm. in Hiezechielem* 16.55 (*CChr* 75, 210, lns. 805-806)

In response Jerome argues that Isaiah 2 refers to the church, which had its origins in the coming of Jesus of Nazareth, not the Messianic age which is anticipated by the Jews. He notes that the term "house" used in Isaiah, "the mountain of the Lord's house," designates the church in the New Testament, for example in 1 Timothy: "You may know how one ought to behave in the household of God, which is the church of the living God, the pillar and bulwark of truth" (3:15). And to respond to the Jewish view that in the Messianic age the nations will come to Jerusalem to do homage to the God of Israel, he argues that this text says that "instruction *shall go forth* out of Zion, and the word of the Lord *from Jerusalem.*" In his view this refers to the spreading of the gospel, which began with the apostles.[58]

Cyril of Alexandria also believed that the key to interpreting the text is the phrase "in the last days," which is to say the "time" to which the text refers. Like John Chrysostom he observes that there is a clean break between the first and second chapters of Isaiah. When the prophet begins chapter two he makes clear that the "vision" of chapter one has come to an end. Now as he records a "second vision" he "designates the time," and that is signified by the phrase "in the last days." The "time" to which the prophet refers is an age in which the power of the devil will be overcome "not in one country and city . . . but in every place under the

---

and 40.5-13 (*CChr* 75, 557, ln. 165). Here he refers to Christ as "Salvator Noster" (467, ln. 57).

58. Jerome, *Comm. in Esaiam* 2.3-4 (*CChr* 73, 29, lns. 40-43). Like Chrysostom, Jerome noted the break between chapters 1 and 2 of isaiah, but because he read the Hebrew text as well as the LXX he also realized that the LXX translators had mistranslated the prepositions in 1.1 and 2.1. In Hebrew the preposition in the phrase "concerning Judah and Jerusalem" is *al,* which means "about" or "concerning." But in the Septuagint 1.1 is rendered "against" *(kata)* and 2.1 "concerning" *(peri).* Jerome comments: *"Miror cur LXX interpretes in illa dixerint: contra Iudaeam et Hierusalem; et in huc: de Iudaea et de Hierusalem . . ."* (*Comm. in Esaiam* 2.1 [*CChr* 73, 26]).

heavens."[59] Because this prophecy has been fulfilled in the birth and expansion of the church into the whole world, the text must be interpreted in light of events that have already taken place. "This [the oracle in Isaiah 2] has been accomplished among those who were on earth in the last days, i.e. at the last times of the present age, in which the only begotten son of God the Word shined forth, born of a woman. . . . Christ showed forth the church of the nations, as it were in the last time, that is at the end of this age" (Heb. 9:26).[60]

Finally Theodoret of Cyrus. Like Chrysostom he notes that chapter two serves almost as "another preface" to the book of Isaiah. The prophet wishes to introduce a different subject from that of chapter one and he signals this by the phrase "in these last days." He observes that the phrase occurs in the New Testament in two key passages. The first is Acts 2:17 where the writer cites Joel 2:28-32: "I will pour out my Spirit on all flesh, and your sons and your daughters shall prophesy. . . . Then everyone who calls on the name of the Lord shall be saved." But in citing the prophet Joel, Acts replaces the opening phrase, "then afterward," with the words of Isaiah, "in these last days." Secondly Theodoret cites Hebrews 1:1: "In many and various ways God spoke to our ancestors by the prophets, but *in these last days* he has spoken to us by a Son."[61]

Accordingly Theodoret interprets the passage with respect to the church, citing Hebrews 3:6, "Christ was faithful over God's *house* as a son, and we are his house," to be a reference to the "Lord's house" in Isaiah 2:2. He also criticizes a purely historical interpretation of the passage. "I am amazed at those who insist

59. Cyril of Alexandria, *Comm. in Isaiam* 2.1 (*PG* 70, 68b).

60. *Comm. in Isaiam* 2.1 (*PG* 70, 68c). Cyril gives a similar interpretation, citing Heb. 9:26, in *Commentary on Micah*. The text refers to the calling of the "church from the gentiles" and to things that happened "among us": *Comm. in Michaeam* 4.1-2 (Pusey, 657).

61. Theodoret of Cyrus, *Comm. in Esaiam* 2.1-2 (*SC* 276, 188-190).

on interpreting this passage otherwise and who think that through these words the return from Babylon was prophesied."[62] Though these observations may have been directed at Jews, it is more likely that Theodoret has in mind Christian interpreters, notably Theodore of Mopsuestia, who, as we have seen, gave the text a strictly historical interpretation.[63] In some places in his commentaries he criticizes Jews who give the prophetic oracles a historical interpretation,[64] but he is more critical of Jews and judaizing Christians who took the restorationist passages of the prophets to be referring to the rebuilding of Jerusalem as a Jewish city.[65]

The ancient oracles of the prophets will inevitably look different when the interpreter is faced with actual events that seem to correspond, however unexpectedly, to what the prophets envisioned.[66] That is true of Jews as well as of Christians. History, even sacred history, seldom follows a predetermined pattern. When the Persians conquered Jerusalem in the seventh century, Jews in Palestine saw the defeat of the Byzantines, that is, the Christians, as a fulfillment of the prophecies about the restoration of Jerusalem. They discerned a close correspondence between the name of the Sassanid Chosroe II and the ancient Persian king Cyrus who had delivered the Jews from the Babylonians.[67] And

---

62. Theodoret of Cyrus, *Comm. in Esaiam* 2.4 (*SC* 276, 192-194).

63. On this point see Jean-Noël Guinot, *Théodoret de Cyr. Commentaire sur Isaïe* (*SC* 276, 193, n. 3).

64. See, for example, Theodoret of Cyrus' *Comm. in Michaeam* 4.1-4 (*PG* 81, 1760d-1761a).

65. See Theodoret of Cyrus, *Comm. in Hiezechielem* 48.35 (*PG* 81, 1248-1256).

66. As Irenaeus puts it: Christ "brought something wholly new *(omnem novitatem)* offering himself who had been announced." To which he adds a few paragraphs later: "For it can be said that none of these things has properly speaking actually happened to any of the fathers or prophets or ancient kings" *(Adv. Haer.* 4.34.1-3).

67. See the Jewish apocalypse *Book of Elijah* in *Midreshei Geulah*, ed. Shmuel, 42.

they saw the words of the prophet coming to fulfillment in their own time.

It is one thing to anticipate a Messianic age at some time in the distant future, something else to claim that it has begun to appear. When that occurs the words of the prophets may not mean what they seem to mean, a point that Maimonides understood well. In his view the Messianic age may not be marked by catastrophic events that make all sit up and take note. When the Messiah comes, he writes, "the world will follow its normal course." For this reason, he says, the words of the prophets, for example, about a peaceable kingdom in Isaiah 11, "the wolf shall live with the lamb, the leopard shall lie down with the kid," are to be taken "figuratively" and "similar expressions used in connection with the Messiah" are to be understood "metaphorically."[68] The meaning of the ancient oracles will only be apparent when the Messianic age has come.

That, finally, was the argument Christian interpreters gave to their critics. The Jews have a much too restricted view of what it means for the prophecies to be fulfilled. Origen cheerfully acknowledged that the words of the prophets have not been fulfilled in the way they were thought to take place. "None of these things that have taken place can be seen with the senses" (*princ.* 4.2.1). Yet something had happened (and was seen) and it had occurred in space and time. The first Christians did not bear witness to an apparition. As Origen put it: "The Word of God itself, that Wisdom of God . . . came to exist within the circumscribed limits of a man who *appeared* in Judea . . ." (*princ.* 2.6.2).

Early Christian interpreters did not impose an evanescent superstructure on the text without root in history or experience. Most Christian exegetes repudiated a literal or historical reading

---

68. Maimonides, *Mishneh Torah,* Book 14, *Book of Judges,* Treatise 5, "Kings and Wars," chap. 12.

of the prophets, not because they preferred allegory or anagogy to history, but because they were attentive to a new set of historical events. If Jesus of Nazareth was the Messiah, as the Scriptures taught, the prophecies about the Messianic age had already been fulfilled, and it was the task of biblical interpreters to discover what the scriptural promises meant in light of this new fact. Paradoxically, in the language of early Christian exegesis, the spiritual sense *was* the historical sense.

6

The Lives of the Saints
and the Pursuit of Virtue

O F THE SEVERAL PATHS that lead to virtue, the broadest
and the most obliging is the way of imitation. By ob-
serving the lives of holy men and women and imitating
their deeds, we become virtuous. Before we can become doers,
we first must be spectators. Origen, the fecund Christian teacher
from ancient Alexandria, said, "Genuine transformation of life
comes from reading the ancient Scriptures, learning who the just
were and *imitating* them," to which he shrewdly appended the
caveat, and "learning who were reproved and guarding against
falling under the same censure."[1]

In a scene in *The Brothers Karamazov*, shortly before Father
Zosima dies, the aged monk gathers his fellow monks and friends
in his cell for a final conversation. As a child he had owned a
book with beautiful pictures entitled *A Hundred and Four Stories
from the Old and the New Testaments*. From this book he had

1. Origen, *Homilies on Jeremiah* 4.5.

Originally published in *New Visions*, ed. Val Ambrose McInnes, O.P. (New
York, 1993), 55-76. Reprinted by permission of Crossroad Publishing Co.

learned to read and, as an old man, he still keeps it on his shelf. Father Zosima remembers many tales from it as well as other stories of good and holy men and women; stories of Job and Esther and Jonah, the parables of Jesus, the conversion of Saul, and lives of the saints Alexel and Mary of Egypt — stories that plant a tiny mysterious seed in the hearts of men and women. Some of these "sacred tales," like the story of Job, he cannot read "without tears." Like a bright spark amidst darkness, or a seed that never dies, these accounts lodge indelibly in his memory. In these stories of God's people, says Father Zosima, one "beh[olds] God's glory." He asks, "What is Christ's word without an example?"[2]

Without examples, without imitation, there can be no human life or civilization, no art or culture, no virtue or holiness. The elementary activities of fashioning a clay pot or constructing a cabinet, learning to speak or sculpting a statue have their beginning in the imitation of what others do. This atavistic truth is as old as humankind, but in the West it was the Greeks who helped us understand its place in the moral life. And in classical antiquity it is nowhere displayed with greater art than in Plutarch's *Lives*.

"Our senses," wrote Plutarch, "apprehend the things they encounter simply because of the impact they make upon us. For this reason the senses must receive everything that presents itself whether it be useful or useless. The mind, however, has the power to turn itself away if it wishes, and readily fasten on what seems best. It is proper, then, that it pursue what is best, so that it may not only behold it but also be nourished by beholding it. . . . Our spiritual vision must be applied to such objects that by their charm invite it to attain its proper good."

Plutarch continued, "Such objects are to be found in *virtuous*

2. From the passage "Of the Holy Writ in the Life of Father Zossima" in Fyodor Dostoevsky, *The Brothers Karamazov*, pt. 1, bk. 6, sect. 2.

deeds; for these implant in those who search them out a zeal and yearning that leads to imitation. In other cases, admiration of the deed does not at once lead to an impulse to do it. Indeed, in many cases the contrary is true. We take delight in what is produced, but have no desire to imitate the one who produced it." We may take pleasure in, for example, the product of a carpenter or factory worker without wanting to be like them. Their actions generate no "ardor in the breast to imitate" their labor, "nor any buoyancy in the soul that arouses zealous impulses to do likewise. But virtue [*arete*] disposes a person so that as soon as one admires the works of virtue one strives to emulate those who performed them. The good things of fortune we love to possess and enjoy, those of virtues we love to perform. . . . The good creates a stir of activity towards itself and implants at once in the spectator an impulse toward action."[3]

In writing the lives of noble Greeks and Romans, Plutarch gave literary form to ideas and conceptions that reached back into Greek antiquity and that continued to exercise a spell over moralists in the early empire. It was a simple yet profound truth, acknowledged by all, even those who chose another vehicle for moral formation. Plutarch's contemporary Seneca, a Stoic philosopher (Plutarch was an eclectic Platonist), wrote letters and moral essays. In one of many letters to Lucilius, a youth he hoped to mold, Seneca wrote: "Plato, Aristotle, and the whole throng of sages . . . derived more benefit from the *character* than from the words of Socrates. The way is long if one follows precepts, but short and accommodating if one imitates examples."[4]

Long before Plutarch and Seneca, Aristotle had shown that the pursuit of virtue is indissolubly bound to deeds, that good actions are not simply the *end* toward which one strives, but the

3. Plutarch, *Life of Pericles* 1-4.
4. Seneca, *Epistulae* 66.

means to reach the goal. It is only through the repeated perfor-mance of good deeds that a virtuous life is possible. In Aristotle's famous formulation, "We become just by doing just acts, temperate by doing temperate acts, brave by doing brave acts."[5] From this conception it was only a short step to the idea that character could be deduced from actions; hence a narrative (selec-tive to be sure) of a person's actions (i.e., a life — *bios* in Greek) was an indulgent instrument for engendering virtue. The philo-sophical grounding for the writing of lives rested on this intimate bond between "deeds" *(praxeis)* and character *(ethos)*.[6] And, as Plutarch recognized, deeds need not mean great and noble dis-plays of bravery or courage. "A slight thing, like a phrase or a jest," he wrote, is often more revealing of character than "battles where thousands fall." For character has to do with constancy and steadiness.[7]

By the time Christianity made its appearance in the Roman Empire, the practice of writing lives was well established.[8] Yet Christian hagiography, if we are to use the later term, did not emerge until the end of the third century and did not burst into luxurious bloom until the fifth. There are, of course, "tales" of heroic men and women in the apocryphal acts of the apostles (as well as in the canonical Acts), and the early acts of the martyrs narrate the "deeds" of a martyr's final hours or days.[9] And most

5. Aristotle, *Nichomachean Ethics* 1103b3.

6. On this point see Albrecht Dihle, *Studien zur Griechischen Biographie,* Abhandlungen der Akademie der Wissenschaften in Goettingen, Phil-hist. Kl, 3 Folge, Nr. 37 (Goettingen, 1970), 57-69.

7. Plutarch, *Alexander* 1.1-2; see Dihle, *Studien,* 62.

8. On "lives in antiquity," see Patricia Cox, *Biography in Late Antiquity* (Berkeley, 1983); Arnaldo Momigliano, *The Development of Greek Biography* (Cam-bridge, 1971); A. Dihle, *Studien;* and Dihle's more recent work, *Die Entstehung der historishen Biographie,* Sitzungsberichte der Heidelberger Akademie der Wis-senscharten, phil. hist. Klasse, 1986, Bericht 3 (Heidelberg, 1987).

9. The Passion of Saint Perpetua and Saint Felicity concludes with these

important of all, there is the life par excellence, the life of Jesus, displayed with subtlety of perception and refinement of feeling in the Gospels, to which I will return shortly.

The initial impression one receives, however, from early Christian literature is that the vehicle of moral instruction is the *precept*.[10] In the earliest Christian writing (1 Thess., for example), Paul said: "You know what *precepts* we gave you through the Lord Jesus. For this is the will of God your sanctification; that you abstain from unchastity; that each one of you know how to take a wife for himself . . . that no man transgress and wrong his brother in this matter." Sprinkled throughout the New Testament are other lists of precepts, some simple imperatives to refrain from "anger, wrath, malice, slander, foul talk," and graceful and polished aphorisms constructed on the model of the book of Proverbs or the *Wisdom of Sirach* ("Let every person be quick to hear, slow to speak, slow to anger") and "If anyone thinks he is religious, and does not bridle his tongue but deceives his heart, this man's religion is vain."[11]

Often the precepts stand alone, but in places they are buttressed by examples: Job as an example of "steadfastness" (James 5:11), Abraham the model of faith (Heb. 11:8), and Elijah as evidence of the power of the prayer of the righteous (James 5:17). In the Gospels Jesus conscripted living persons as examples, a certain poor widow who offered a farthing, little children, Mary of Bethany, the centurion whose slave was at the point of death, and, of course, he told stories and parables, sometimes ending with the words: "Go thou and do likewise" (Luke 10:37). From

---

words: "These examples [*exempla*] too should be read aloud for the building up of the church" (21).

10. On the parenetic tradition in early Christianity, see Wayne Meeks, *The Moral World of the First Christians* (Philadelphia, 1988).

11. Col. 3:8; James 1:19, 27.

the beginning the idea of imitation shaped Christian moral discourse.[12] Paul entreated the Corinthians to take him as an example: "I urge you, then, be imitators of me" (1 Cor. 4:16). Long before the advent of Christianity, the principle was endorsed by Jews, in, for example, the roll call of heroes in the section "let us now praise famous men" in the *Wisdom of Sirach* (44ff.). In Christianity the book of Hebrews unfolds a roster of men and women of faith in chapter eleven — Abel, Enoch, Noah, Abraham, Sarah, Moses, Rahab, Gideon — and 1 Clement produces another list.[13]

Examples, however, are not lives. In the case of the biblical heroes, holy men and women tend to function more as types, that is, instances of particular virtues, than as iridescent models. In Ambrose's classical work on Christian ethics, *De Officiis,* Abraham illustrates prudence; Susanna, modesty; David, courage; Job, patience.[14] Stripped of the grainy texture of place and time, the saints of the distant past become pallid and lackluster, mobilized too often for too many different purposes. As graphic as the saints' deeds may once have been, repeated appeal to the same figures divests them of the very features that once made them noteworthy, severing the emotional bond between doer and spectator.

Why, then, no lives? The most obvious reason was that the Gospels stood in the way. The supreme model for Christian life was Jesus: "I have given you an example that you also should do as I have done" (John 13:15). Even those whose exploits would

---

12. H. Crouzel, "L'Imitation et la 'suite' de Dieu et du Christ dans les premiers siècles chrétiens, ainsi que leur sources gréco-romaines et hébraïques," *Jahrbuch für Antike und Christentum* 21 (1978): 7-41.

13. *Wisdom of Sirach,* chapter 44ff. 1 Clement 9; see also 1 Clement 5:1, 16:17; 46:2.

14. See Ambrose, *De Officiis* 1.117; 68; 113; 177. For Ambrose, however, the several virtues are made to fit, willy-nilly, almost any biblical hero.

have been fit subjects for a life — most notably Peter and Paul (an idea the author of Acts no doubt contemplated, and in part executed) — looked to Jesus. "Be imitators of me," wrote Paul, "as I am of Christ" (1 Cor. 11:1). Others followed in this wake. Ignatius of Antioch exhorted the Philadelpians "to imitate Jesus Christ as he imitated the Father." Jesus' call to discipleship, "Follow me" (Mark 1:16) was an imperative to model one's life on his. Clement of Alexandria expressed it at the end of the second century: "Our tutor Jesus exemplifies the true life and trains the one who is in Christ. . . . He gives commands and embodies the commands that we might be able to accomplish them."[15]

The very existence of the Gospels served as a deterrent to the writing of lives of other holy persons. In them was to be found the noblest example of all. At this stage of Christian history, it would have been presumptuous to bring other persons into competition with the primal model. Only after Nicaea did the need arise for other exemplars. It should be remembered that the most potent arrows in the quiver of the Arians were those passages in the Gospels that spoke of Jesus' human features, his limited knowledge, his obedience to God, his growth in wisdom (improvability), his suffering.[16] Once it was declared that the Logos was "of one substance with the Father" (defended chiefly by appeal to the Gospel of John), a vacuum was created that could be filled with other human faces.

Whatever the historical explanation for the rise of Christian hagiography, by the early fourth century Christians began to discover within their midst the human and spiritual resources to embark on a new strategy for teaching virtue. The first intimations of a new way are visible in the relations forged between master

15. Ignatius of Antioch, *Phil.* 7.12; Clement of Alexandria, *paed.* 1.12.98.1-3; also 1 Clement 1:8.

16. On this point, see Robert C. Gregg and Dennis E. Groh, *Early Arianism — A View of Salvation* (Philadelphia, 1981), 1-30.

and disciple within the Christian community in the second and third centuries. In the ancient world moral education was private and individual, based on a master-disciple relation that was nurtured through bonds of friendship, respect, and admiration; according to Peter Brown, "No student ever went, as we do, to a university conceived of as an impersonal institution of learning. . . . He would always have gone to a person — to Libanius, to Origen, to Proclus."[17] When Gregory the wonderworker came to Caesarea to study with Origen, he wanted, in his words, "to have fellowship with this man" and through him to be transformed. By establishing an intimate personal bond with the student, Origen awakened in him the desire for a new life. The cement of this union was "love," and Gregory says that it was only when he was "smitten" by Origen's love that he was persuaded to give up "those objects that stood in the way of practicing the virtuous life." What goaded the disciple to change was not exhortation but deeds: "He exhorted us by his actions and incited us more by what he did than by what he said."[18]

Gregory did not write a life of Origen, but his "appreciation" of Origen provides a bridge to the first Christian lives. At about the same time that Gregory wrote his essay, Pontus, a disciple of Cyprian, composed what may be considered the first Christian "saint's life." His *Vita et Passio Cypriani*, written shortly after Cyprian's death as a martyr (ca. 259 C.E.), is the work of a man who had served as deacon under the great bishop and knew him well.[19]

17. Peter Brown, "The Saint as Exemplar in Late Antiquity," in *Saints and Virtues*, ed. John Stratton Hawley (Berkeley, 1987), 4.

18. Gregory Thaumaturgus, *Panegyric* 5.70; 6.81; 9.123. For discussion (and bibliography), see Robert L. Wilken, "Alexandria: A School for Training in Virtue," in *Schools of Thought in the Christian Tradition*, ed. Patrick Henry (Philadelphia, 1984), 15-30.

19. Pontus, *Vita et Passio Cypriani*, ed. A. von Harnack, *Texte und Untersuchungen* 39.3 (Leipzig, 1913).

A more conventional disciple would have written Cyprian's final days in the style of other "acts of the martyrs," a popular literary genre among Christians in North Africa (and elsewhere). Here was a proven form to celebrate the deeds of a holy person in bright and colorful detail. Pontus, however, consciously broke with this tradition. Cyprian, he explained, "had much to teach, *independently* of his martyrdom; what he did *while* he lived should not be hidden from the world." Pontus' purpose in writing the *Vita,* he said, was to hold up the "lofty pattern" *(documentum)* that was displayed in the "actions" and "accomplishments" of Cyprian's entire life, not only his courage at the time of his martyrdom. These deeds, too, were worthy of preservation in "eternal memory."[20]

Although Pontus eschewed the convention of depicting only the final feats of his hero, in one significant respect he stood within the earlier tradition: He wrote about someone he knew at firsthand, not about a hero from the distant past.[21] His life told of a man he loved and admired and who had formed Pontus' own life. The *Vita* summons forth the memories of those who had known Cyprian for years, those who had lived and worked with him, as well as those who had been spectators of his final testimony, his martyrdom.

To a certain extent Pontus' *Vita* was premature. It would be a hundred years before Athanasius wrote the *Life of Antony.* The *Passio et Vita Cypriani,* however, locates a path for us between Christian ethical teaching in the second and third centuries and the works of the fourth and fifth centuries, the great age of Christian hagiography. It foreshadows a development that would alter the face of Christian literature and piety. For with the pub-

---

20. *Vita Cypriani* 1.

21. The author of the Passion of Saint Perpetua and Saint Felicity said that these new displays of virtue *(novae virtutes)* were "not less precious than the examples of old" *(non minora veteribus exempla)* (21). Contrast, for example, the lives of Abraham or Joseph written by Philo, or Gregory of Nyssa's *Life of Moses.*

lication and rapid dissemination of the *Life of Antony*, a new era began. To give but a partial list of the many works that appeared during the next three hundred years testifies to the vitality and breadth of this tradition in the generations after the *Life of Antony*: *Life of Pachomius*, Palladius' *Life of John Chrysostom*, Gerontius' *Life of Melania* (first full life of a woman ascetic), John Rufus' *Life of Peter the Iberian*, Theodoret of Cyrus' *Religious History*, Cyril of Scythopolis' *Lives of Palestinian Monks*, Sulpicius Severus' *Life of Martin of Tours*, John of Ephesus' *Lives of the Eastern Saints*.[22]

Now these works are many and varied. Some are written in an elegant and refined style, self-consciously contraposing Christian saints to the heroes of Greek and Latin antiquity; others are homespun and unaffected tales, ignorant or disdainful of the conventions of the literary culture. Some works dwell on the eccentric and grotesque, men who sat for years on pillars or who lived in huts too narrow to stretch out in; some read like romances and adventure stories; some depict fierce inner struggles; others describe unexceptional acts of mercy or almsgiving; some are frankly apologetic, using the life of the saint to defend a particular theological position (e.g., the christological formulas of Chalcedon) or the view of its critics.

22. Many of these "lives" are available in English translations: *The Life of Pachomius*, trans. Apostolos N. Athanassakis (Missoula, 1975); Gerontius, *The Life of Melania the Younger*, trans. Elizabeth A. Clark (New York, 1984); Theodoret of Cyrus, *A History of the Monks of Syria*, trans. R. M. Price (Kalamazoo, 1985); Sulpicius Severus et al., *The Western Fathers*, trans. F. R. Hoare (New York, 1954); Sebastian P. Brock and Susan Ashbrook Harvey, *Holy Women of the Syrian Orient* (Berkeley, 1987); Elizabeth Dawes and Norman H. Baynes, *Three Byzantine Saints* (Crestwood, N.Y., 1977). In the sixth and seventh centuries, there was also a proliferation of portraits of holy persons. See Ernest Kitzinger, "Christian Imagery: Growth and Impact," in *Age of Spirituality: A Symposium*, ed. Kurt Weitzmann (Princeton, 1980), 149, and E. Kitzinger, *Late Classical and Mediaeval Studies in Honor of Albert Matthias Friend, Jr.* (Princeton, 1955), 132-150.

With few exceptions, two features characterize all these lives. First, they hold up "imitation" as the path to virtue. In the *Life of Antony,* Athanasius wrote: "Simply by seeing Antony's conduct many desired to become imitators."[23] Theodoret of Cyrus, in the preface to his *Religious History* (of the holy men and women of Syria), explained that he was writing down these lives so that others may "imitate" them.[24] The proper subject of the lives are "deeds," not sayings (though they include sayings), that is, actions that can be emulated or at least admired and venerated. In a letter placed at the beginning of his *Lausiac History,* Palladius wrote: "Words and syllables do not constitute teaching. . . . Teaching consists of virtuous acts of conduct. . . . This is how Jesus taught. . . . He did not use fine language . . . he required the formation of character."[25] As is to be expected in works that focus on actions, the lives prize "seeing" over "hearing." The saints are "living icons." A constant refrain is that the author wrote of what he had "seen with his own eyes."[26]

It is only by seeing that one can take the measure of a person's character and remember what one has learned; that is, have the saint's character imprinted on one's mind and soul. John of Lycopolis wrote: "We have come to you from Jerusalem for the good of our souls, so that what we have heard with our ears we might perceive with our eyes — for the ears are naturally less reliable than the eyes — and because very often forgetfulness follows what we heard, whereas the memory of what we have

23. Athanasius, *Life of Antony* 46. In the introduction, Athanasius wrote "Since you have asked me about the way of life of the blessed Antony, hoping to learn how he began the discipline, who he was before this, and what sort of death he experienced, and if the things said concerning him are true — so that you also might lead yourselves in *imitation of him* — I received your directive with ready good will."

24. Theodoret of Cyrus, *Religious History* 1-3.

25. Palladius, *The Lausiac History* 1-2, ed. Robert T. Meyer (New York, 1964).

26. Theodoret, *Religious History* 2, 11; 21.5.

seen is not easily erased but remains imprinted on our minds like a picture."[27] As Plutarch recognized, it is sight, visual images formed in the imagination, that has the power to excite in people the desire for emulation.[28]

Second, the subjects of the "lives" are men and women the author knew or about whom reliable information was available from people who knew them. "I write," said Theodoret, about "the glorious saints of our own time and the recent past."[29] The lives bear the hues and colors of the communities that produced them. Theodoret calls one of the saints from Cyrus the "fruit of Cyrus."[30] The protagonists are not figures from the past, heroes sanitized by tradition, but gnarly contemporaries. The lives were written as a hedge against forgetfulness of what had taken place in one's midst and in one's "own time." Neither are these tales of kings and generals, and seldom do they depict clergy. Most of the heroes are laymen and laywomen. Indeed one of the stock temptations is the lure of ordination, an enticement the best always resist. The lives are stories of simple and unassuming men and women who love God more ardently and serve God more zealously than their neighbors and friends, the kinds of persons who are present in every Christian community, indeed in every religious community.

27. John of Lycopolis, *Historia Monachorum* 19, ET in *The Lives of the Desert Fathers,* ed. and trans. Benedicta Ward and Norman Russell (London, 1981), 54-55.

28. In his life of Symeon the Fool, Leontius, bishop of Neapolis in Cyprus, wrote: "For those who are zealously devoted in soul to God, *conscience* is a sufficient basis for teaching. It exhorts us to do good things and diverts us from evil things. To those who are more humble than these, there is need of the *precepts* of the law and exhortation. If, however, someone slips through the first or second way which leads to virtue, such a one can only be aroused to desire God . . . and to pursue the hard and difficult way, by the zeal and devotion of those whose lives he sees or about whom he hears a story" (*Patrologia Graeca* 93.1669-1671).

29. Theodoret, *Religious History* 1.1.

30. Theodoret, *Religious History* 17.2.

Of course the "lives" include stereotypical scenes — the vision of a temptress on the wall of a cave, the wounded lion befriended by the gentle monk, the master gathering his disciples in anticipation of his death — and the portraits are often highly idealized. Yet the fabric of these works bears the imprint of the unique personality of the subject more than the marks of traditional literary conventions or the author's conception of what constitutes a virtuous life. The hagiographers did not offer a grocery list of virtues. The individual life, like the living master, generates its own "criterion for evaluation."[31] The hagiographers wrote about the real accomplishments of living men and women, about deeds that were remembered and admired and evoked to display the saint's unique character, not to illustrate or exemplify a virtue or set of virtues. They filled the space left vacant by the departure of the master.

Once the deeds of virtuous men and women were set within the framework of a life, in contrast to disembodied examples, the possibilities for moral instruction became more subtle and varied.[32] For one thing the hagiographer could exploit the passage

31. The phrase is from A. S. Cua, *Dimensions of Moral Creativity: Paradigms, Principles and Ideals* (University Park, 1978), 40.

32. In defending her preference for "tragedies" over "examples" to illuminate moral action, Martha Nussbaum (in *The Fragility of Goodness, Luck and Ethics in Greek Tragedy and Philosophy* [Cambridge, 1986], 14) writes: "We can say provisionally that a whole tragic drama, unlike a schematic philosophical example making use of a similar story, is capable of tracing the history of a complex pattern of deliberation, showing its roots in a way of life and looking forward to its consequences in that life. As it does all of this, it lays open to view the complexity, the indeterminacy, the sheer difficulty of actual human deliberation. If a philosopher were to use Antigone's story as a philosophical example, he or she would, in setting it out schematically, signal to the reader's attention everything that the reader ought to notice. He would point out what is strictly relevant. A tragedy does not display the dilemmas of its characters as pre-articulated; it shows them searching for the morally salient; and it forces us, as interpreters, to be similarly active. Interpreting a tragedy is a messier, less determinate, more mysterious matter than

of time. No one becomes virtuous in a few weeks or months; holiness is only learned gradually, over a long period of time. True virtue requires years, decades of guidance, discipline, prayer, and acts of charity. When Sabas, the architect of Palestinian monasticism, comes to Euthymius in the desert east of Jerusalem, he has already excelled in virtue in his homeland Cappadocia; yet when he asks Euthymius, the seer of the Judaean desert, if he can become his disciple, Euthymius says that Sabas is too young (he is eighteen) to adopt the solitary life. He puts him under the care of another monk, Theoctistus, who will lead him in the first steps of monastic discipline. Serving first as muleteer, Sabas gradually takes on whatever other tasks are required. Only after twelve years, when Sabas has reached the age of thirty, is he given permission to live alone, on the condition that he return each week on Saturday and Sunday to the main house. Eventually he is allowed to become a genuine solitary, but it is not until he is forty-five years old that he is entrusted with the direction of other monks.[33]

Spiritual progress is measured not in weeks or months, but in years, even in decades. Twenty, thirty, in some cases forty years is not uncommon. Saint Antony lives by himself for twenty years, "not venturing out and only occasionally being seen by anyone." Only at the end of this time, when his soul has achieved "utter equilibrium," is he ready to accept disciples.[34] Dwelling on the passage of time highlights the value of constancy or steadfastness (in Aristotle's vocabulary, "stability"). "Acting in accord with

---

assessing a philosophical example; and even when the work has once been interpreted, it remains unexhausted, subject to reassessment, in a way that the example does not."

33. Cyril of Scythopolis, *Life of Sabas,* ed. Eduard Schwartz, *Texte und Untersuchungen* 49 (Leipzig, 1939); ET by R. M. Price, *Lives of the Monks of Palestine* by Cyril of Scythopolis (Kalamazoo, 1991).

34. Athanasius, *Life of Antony* 14, trans. Robert Gregg (New York, 1980), 42.

virtue," wrote Aristotle, "must occupy a lifetime. For one swallow does not make spring nor does one fine day summer."[35]

Instead of a single deed there are repeated deeds. Apollonius, a businessman who has renounced the world to live in the Nitrian desert, devotes all his energies to one task. With his own medicine and groceries, he provides for those who are sick: "He could be seen making his round of the monasteries from early morn to the ninth hour, going in door after door to find out if anyone was sick. He used to bring grapes and pomegranates, eggs and cakes such as the sick fancy." This way of life, reported the hagiographer, he practices faithfully and without interruption for *twenty years*.[36]

The "lives" accentuate habit, the constant performance of good deeds, as the condition for progress in virtue. In modern times no one has expressed this insight more clearly than William James in his *Principles of Psychology:*

> Could the young but realize how soon they will become mere walking bundles of habits, they could give more heed to their conduct while in the plastic state. . . . Every smallest stroke of virtue or vice leaves its never so little scar. The drunken Rip van Winkle, in Jefferson's play, excuses himself for every fresh dereliction by saying, "I won't count this time." Well! He may not count it, and a kind of heaven may not count it; but it is being counted none the less. Down among his nerve-cells and fibres the molecules are counting it, registering and storing it up to be used against him when the second temptation comes. . . . As we become permanent drunkards by so many separate drinks, so we become saints in the moral . . . sphere by so many separate acts.[37]

35. Aristotle, *Nichomachean Ethics* 1098a115-116.
36. Palladius, *Lausiac History* 13, pp. 48-49.
37. William James, *The Principles of Psychology* (New York, 1910), 127.

In contrast to the appeal to stock examples, "lives" also make a place for the unpredictable and novel. At times it may be nothing more than the playful addition of stray detail to the narrative. Theodore of Sykeon (who spends his time in a cage suspended out over the face of a cliff) is said to have been a swift runner. Several times on a wager he ran a race of three miles with horses and beat them.[38] But more often the unexpected is purposeful, designed to show that the hero is free of the comfortable expectations of society, and enlarges the moral horizon of the hearer.

Marcianos is visited by an older monk, Avitos, who lives in another part of the desert. When Avitos arrives, Marcianos' friend boils some vegetables and greens. After the vegetables have been cooked, Marcianos says to Avitos, "Come my dear friend, let us have fellowship together at the table." But Avitos responds: "I don't think I have ever eaten before evening. I often pass two or three days in succession without taking anything." Marcianos (the younger) replies (not without irony), "On my account change your custom today for my body is weak and I am not able to wait until evening." But even that cannot convince Avitos. Marcianos sighs and says, "I am disheartened and my soul is stung because you have expended much effort to come and look at a true ascetic; but instead you are disappointed and behold a tavern keeper and profligate instead of an ascetic." Finally Avitos relents, and Marcianos says: "My dear friend. We both share the same existence and embrace the same way of life, we prefer work to rest, fasting to nourishment, and it is only in the evening that we eat, but we know that love is a much more precious possession than fasting. For the one is the work of divine law, the other of our own power. And it is proper to consider the divine law much more precious than our own." Theodoret, com-

---

38. *Life of Theodore of Sykeon* 13, trans. Elizabeth Dawes and Norman H. Baynes (Crestwood, N.Y., 1977), 13.

menting on this virtuous deed, observes that Marcianos knows there is a time for fasting and a time for Christian fellowship. He knows how "to distinguish the different parts of virtue, what can step aside for another, and when to give preference to something else because of the circumstances."[39]

In his *Life of Euthymius,* Cyril of Scythopolis recorded another story with an unexpected ending (in light of what one has already learned about his hero). Euthymius is a recluse, and his entire life is marked by a quest for complete solitude *(hesychia).* Yet no matter how deep into the desert he withdraws, people follow him. His life is a story of constant flight to different parts of the Judaean desert, even to the top of Masada (before there was a cable car). His is a stern and uncompromising asceticism, whose chief marks are obedience, fasting, mastery of the passions, solitude. Yet when Euthymius, the great solitary, is about to die, those practices are not the things he speaks of. One year at the feast of Epiphany, a time when Euthymius usually sets off for the "outer desert" to return only at Easter, he does not make his usual preparations. Puzzled, his disciples ask him why. He answers cryptically, "I will remain here this week and on Saturday at night I will leave" (announcing his own death). Three days later he calls his disciples together and addresses them as follows: "My beloved brothers, I go the way of my fathers. If you love me keep these commandments. Hold fast through everything to sincere love which is the beginning and end of all doing of good and the bond of perfection. Just as it is not possible to eat bread without salt, so it is impossible to practice virtue without love. All virtue is established through love and humility by experience and time and grace. Humility, however, exalts . . . since the one who humbles himself will be exalted. . . . Love is greater than humility."[40]

39. Theodoret, *Religious History* 3.12.
40. Cyril of Scythopolis, *Life of Euthymius* 39.

The Life of Euthymius says little of love. Even in the summary of teaching elsewhere in the book, Euthymius does not mention love. According to his biographer, the marks of the monastic vocation are meditation, discernment of spirits, temperance, and obedience.[41] Yet at his death Euthymius speaks only on communal virtues, of the bonds of fellowship, of mutual love.

The lives, then, do not present a single ideal of virtue, nor do they offer one paradigm of holiness. They recognize and recommend different ways of pursuing the goal of perfection, focusing less on traditional virtues than on the unique qualities of a particular person. By displaying how a single person responded to new and varied situations, these stories implicitly suggest that there is no single standard, no one catalogue of virtues, no one way to serve God.

One account deals with two sons of a Spanish merchant. When their father dies, they divide the estate, which consists of five thousand coins, clothes, and slaves, and the sons deliberate on how they should deal with this wealth. Neither wants to be a merchant. Each wants to live a holy life, but they disagree as to what form that should take. So they divide the property and go their separate ways. Paesius gives away everything he has — to the churches, the monasteries, and the prisons — learns a trade to provide for his own needs, and devotes himself to a solitary life of prayer. Isaias keeps the wealth, builds a monastery, takes in some brothers, and welcomes the poor, setting three or four tables on Saturday and Sunday. When the two men die, a dispute arises as to who had chosen the better way. Some claim Paesius excelled because he had hearkened to the command in the gospel to "sell all you have" and follow Jesus (Luke 18:22); others say that Isaias was the greater because he had served others. But Pambo, a wise, old monk, says, "Both are equal." Pambo has had

41. Cyril of Scythopolis, *Life of Euthymius* 9.

a dream in which he "saw both of them standing in paradise in the presence of God."[42]

Other writers draw an even sharper antithesis between contrasting ways of life. Maesymas is a Syriac-speaking peasant with no education. At first he pursues the solitary life in the desert, but later he comes to live in a village. Unlike the other ascetic stars in Theodoret of Cyrus' collection of lives, Maesymas does not sit on a pillar, he does not live in the "open air," he does not weight down his body with chains. He gives himself to the needs of his fellow villagers: "His doors were always open to passers by." Like the widow of Zarephath who fed Elijah, said Theodoret, Maesymas' jar of grain and pitcher of oil are always full. Recognizing that Maesymas does not conform to the conventional picture of a "godly man," Theodoret explained: "Many other stories of this kind are told about this godly person. One can learn from them that those who choose to live virtuously are harmed not at all by life in towns and villages; for this man and those like him responsible for the service of God have shown that it is possible even for those who go about among many to attain the very summit of the virtues."[43] This was quite an admission in an age when the solitary life was the zenith of sanctity.

Theodoret, however, may have felt his praise of Maesymas to be excessive because he followed his "life" with the tale of one of the true eccentrics: Acepsimas. Theodoret described Acepsimas: "Shutting himself up in a cell, he remained there for sixty years without being seen and without speaking." He has taken to heart the words of the psalm: "Take delight in the Lord." Acepsimas

---

42. Palladius, *Lausiac History* 14. Other stories make a similar point. The anchorite Paphnutius, after hearing of the good deeds of a practitioner of the despised occupation of flute playing, said, "I am not aware myself of having accomplished anything equal to this" (John of Lycopolis, *Historia Monachorum* 14; trans. Ward and Russell, 95).

43. Theodoret, *Religious History* 14.

receives food — lentils soaked in water — by stretching his hand through a small hole. Theodoret explained, "To prevent himself from being exposed to those who wished to see him, the hole was not dug straight through the thickness of the wall, but obliquely, being made in the shape of a curve."[44] So holy was Acepsimas that when he died everyone tried to seize his body and carry it off to his own village. The lives of these holy people do not conform to a predetermined pattern. The saint, like a plant that bends and twists to receive the sun, follows the course of God, always turning to the light that is the source of life.

Not only do the "lives" offer the unexpected — saints who do not always conform to stock virtues or conventional patterns — they also put a new figure on the stage, the holy woman. There had always been female models — Sarah, Naomi, Judith, Rahab, Mary, Felicity, and Perpetua — but as Christian hagiography matured more and more women became the subjects of lives, and their exploits took on new visibility and significance for Christian piety. As has been observed often in recent years, the early Christian monastic movement offered women a way to step free of inherited roles and expectations,[45] and the hagiographers seized the opportunity to tell their stories, some of which are as spellbinding as those of their male counterparts. Melania, for example, is a more extreme ascetic than many men. She wishes to fast even on Easter, she sleeps in sackcloth, and she has a box constructed for sleeping in which she can neither stretch out nor turn over.[46]

What becomes apparent at once in reading the lives of holy

44. Theodoret, *Religious History* 15.

45. See Elizabeth A. Clark, *Ascetic Piety and Women's Faith* (New York, 1986).

46. *Life of Melania* 25, 31, 32. Before she gave birth to her son (stillborn), she spent the night in the chapel kneeling and keeping vigil (5). The Latin version of the life says that Melania's father sent eunuchs to make certain she was in her room sleeping. Melania bribed them so they would not tell her father where she was.

women is that they do not cultivate "feminine" virtues. Sylvania, for example, is "erudite and fond of literature" (a kind of patron saint for female seminarians); day and night she reads the ancient Christian commentators, three million lines of Origen and two and a half million lines of Gregory, Basil, and others. She is liberated from "knowledge falsely so called" and is able "to mount on wings . . . and by good hopes she transformed herself into a spiritual bird and so made the journey to Christ."[47] Another woman, Susan, contends with demons. Once she is visited by a "blessed man, great and God-loving," who lives in the desert nearby. Each observes the other in combat with demons. Susan, however, is "stronger than he. She not only conquered the demons, she had no fear of them. She became firm like adamant and unmoveable — so much that the demons would cry out at her, 'This is a woman, but she is stone, and instead of flesh she is iron!' "[48]

The hagiographers' attribution of remarkable feats to women contradicted the popular view that women's capacity for virtue was inferior to that of men. "I must commemorate the courageous women to whom God granted struggles equal to those of men so that no one could plead as an excuse that women are too weak to practice virtue successfully. I have seen a good many of them."[49] Theodoret of Cyrus echoed that idea: "Virtue cannot be separated into male and female. . . . For the difference is one of bodies not of souls," and as the Scripture says, "in Christ Jesus . . . there is neither male nor female. . . . Women too may be models of the virtuous life."[50]

47. Palladius, *Lausiac History* 55.
48. Brock and Harvey, *Holy Women of the Syrian Orient*, 140.
49. Palladius, *Lausiac History* 41.
50. Theodoret, *Religious History* 30. Theodoret of Cyrus cites Gal. 3:28: "There is neither Jew nor Greek, there is neither slave nor free, there is neither male nor female." A similar point is made by John of Ephesus in his lives of Mary

In places the hagiographers allow the reader, though infrequently and exiguously, to glimpse the hero's shortcomings.[51] The saints are not perfect; saints are made, not born. They are impulsive, they backslide, they fall into temptation, they are petty and prideful, they lack self-discipline. A monk at the lavra of Gerasimos in the Jordan valley goes to the abbot and says, "Father, I want to leave the place where I live, because I am very bored."[52] And Conon, a monk in the Jordan valley charged with the responsibility of baptizing, is nonetheless embarrassed and wants to leave the monastery when he has to baptize women. Saint John (the baptizer) appears to Conon and says, "Be patient, I will deliver you from that struggle." Shortly afterward a beautiful Persian maiden comes to be baptized. Conon cannot baptize her. The bishop, Peter, says that he will have a deaconess baptize the maiden. Conon, however, wants to continue in his office. So he goes off by himself for prayer, and again John the Baptizer appeared to him. "Return," he said, "to your monastery and I will deliver you from the struggle." This time Conun replied, "Listen here, I'm not going back. You've often made

---

and Euphemia: "Since we learn from the divine Paul who said, 'In Christ Jesus there is neither male nor female,' it seemed to us that we should introduce the story of those who are by nature females, since mention of them in no way lessens this series of stories about holy men. Furthermore, their course of life was not lower than the exalted path upon which every one of these holy men has journeyed, and even their way of life was great and surpasses telling" (Brock and Harvey, *Holy Women of the Syrian Orient*, 124).

51. Shortcomings are revealed only up to a point. The hagiographers are chary of criticizing their heroes. By contrast, Jews felt no such constraints. An instructive case is the difference in the portrait of Joseph by Christians (e.g., Ambrose's *De Josepho*) and that by Jews (e.g., in *Genesis Rabbah* 84.51). I am indebted for this point to a seminar paper presented at the University of Virginia by Margaret Mohrmann. For a discussion of why "sainthood" has played a minor role in Judaism, see Robert L. Cohn, "Sainthood on the Periphery: The Case of Judaism," in *Saints and Virtues*, 87-110.

52. John Moschus, *Pratrum Spirituale*, 142.

promises to me and not kept them." St. John threw him to the ground, pulled up his habit, marked his stomach with three crosses, and told him to take courage and go ahead with the baptism. So Conun returned to the monastery, baptized the maiden, anointed her with oil, and, adds the hagiographer, his body did not move.[53]

The lives, then, do much more than provide a model to imitate. They arouse, judge, inspire, challenge, surprise, amuse, and excite the reader. Their authors do not simply set down a minimalist standard for all to imitate. Indeed, many of the specific things they portray are beyond imitation, at least for ordinary mortals. They point beyond the familiar and prosaic to a higher and more noble vision of the Christian life.[54] One of the most cited biblical texts was Philippians 3:13: "I forget what lies behind and strain forward to what lies ahead." What lay ahead, however, could not be specified for everyone without distinction; the goal was not the same for all. The lives of the saints, in Karl Jasper's words, serve more as "beacons by which to gain an orientation" than as "models for imitation."[55] Not everyone can or will pursue the same path. The criteria for judging virtue and holiness vary.

The lives of the saints do not present us with a new theory of virtue, but a new way of teaching virtue, a new strategy that builds on the tradition of examples, but enriches it by displaying a pattern of holiness over the course of a lifetime.

53. *Pratrum Spirituale*, 3.

54. Iris Murdoch writes: "In assessing people we do not consider only response to particular problems, but look for their total vision as shown in their mode of speech or silence, their choice of words, their assessments of others, their conceptions of their own lives, what they think attractive or praiseworthy . . . in short, the configurations of their thought which show continually in their reactions and conversations" ("Vision and Choice in Morality," in Paul Ramsey, ed., *Christian Ethics and Contemporary Philosophy* [New York, 1966], 202).

55. Karl Jaspers, *Socrates, Buddha, Confucius, and Jesus: The Four Paradigmatic Individuals* (New York, 1957), 96.

Precepts are now put in the mouths of familiar persons, and examples are enhanced by seeing them as deeds of specific individuals. The hagiographers, for the first time in Christian history, turn to living persons, or those who have recently died, as models of the virtuous life. There is a great boldness here, to choose people from one's midst, to hold up to view peasants and farmers and jugglers and sailors, even bishops, presenting them as models for their neighbors, fellow citizens, and friends. By displaying men and women from their own time, and often from their own communities, these lives proclaim: holiness is possible, virtue is attainable, perfection is within your grasp. They teach, in Bergson's phrase, a morality of aspiration not of obligation.[56] By placing before our eyes deeds that provoke, excite, and charm the ignorant and the educated alike, women and men, city dwellers and farmers, soldiers and kings and merchants, the lives of the saints set us on a sure path toward holiness.

56. Henri Bergson, *Two Sources of Morality* (New York, 1935), 43. See also Kai Nielson, "Why Should I Be Moral," in Paul Taylor, ed., *Problem of Moral Philosophy* (1967), 516. Nielson states, "For the most part, people get their standards not from ethical treatises or even scriptural texts or homely sayings, but by idealizing and following the example of some living person or persons."

7

Loving God
with a Holy Passion

JONATHAN EDWARDS begins his treatise *The Religious Affections* with a citation from 1 Peter 1:8: "Whom having not seen, ye love; in whom, though now ye see him not, yet believing, ye rejoice with joy unspeakable and full of glory." What drew Edwards to this passage were the phrases "ye love" and "ye rejoice with joy unspeakable." For Edwards, "love" and "joy" were affections, and his book was a defense of the view that "true religion" consisted not only in "actings of the inclination and will of the soul" but also in "the fervent exercises of the heart." The religion that God requires has nothing to do with a "state of indifference," he writes, but rather has to do with ardor, with a fervent spirit and a burning heart, in short, with passions of the soul. "The holy Scriptures," he writes, "do everywhere place religion very much in the affections; such as fear, hope, love, hatred, desire, joy, sorrow, gratitude, compassion, and zeal."[1]

1. Jonathan Edwards, *The Religious Affections* (Carlisle, Penn., 1984), 21-31.

Previously unpublished paper presented at an international conference on asceticism at Union Theological Seminary, New York, N.Y., April 1993.

The writings of Jonathan Edwards may seem a strange place to begin a discussion of Maximus the Confessor (d. 662). One of these two men was a Congregationalist pastor, married, a revivalist preacher, the other a Byzantine monk, a recluse who believed that *apatheia*, freedom from passion, was the goal of the spiritual life. The true Christians, writes Maximus, are those "who pass beyond the disturbances brought about by the passions."[2] Yet, as several distinguished interpreters of Maximus have observed, Maximus did not counsel, as had the Stoics, that the passions be eradicated. Rather, Maximus speaks of transforming the passions to put them at the service of love.[3] It is perhaps more than coincidental that the two terms that Jonathan Edwards singles out, "love" and "joy," are biblical words for the two affections, desire and delight, that figure large in Maximus's presentation of the spiritual life.

Maximus begins his great work *Quaestiones ad Thalassium*, a dense book dealing with difficult texts from the Bible, with the question of whether the passions are evil in themselves or whether they become evil through their use. His answer is that without the affections it is not possible to hold fast to virtue and knowledge, that is, to cling to God. No doubt it is because of Maximus's penetrating grasp of the turbulent and capricious emotions that he has been venerated by spiritual and ascetical writers in the past and is today being read with keen interest. He is a sensitive interpreter of human experience, not simply a speculative thinker. As Christoph von Schoenborn observed at the Maximus symposium in 1980, Maximus has "a freshness" that endears him to twentieth-century readers.[4]

---

2. Maximus, *Quaestiones ad Thalassium*, ed. Carl Laga and Carlos Steel, *Corpus Christianorum*, Series Graeca, No. 7 (Turnhout, 1980), p. 21, lns. 71-72; also *Quaest. Thal.* 55, p. 489, lns. 144-145.

3. See Irénée Hausherr, S.J., *Philautie. De la Tendresse pour soi à la Charité selon Saint Maxime le Confesseur* (Rome, 1952), 145-146.

4. Christoph von Schoenborn, "Plaisir et douleur dans l'analyse de S. Max-

The topic of the passions enters Christian thought within the context of ethics or moral philosophy. In addressing the topic of the passions (or affections), Christian thinkers joined a discussion that had been going on for centuries.[5] From the outset it is apparent not only that they are well aware of positions staked out by Greek and Roman philosophers but also that, in light of the Scriptures and Christian experience, they had to take sides on matters that had been debated by Greek and Roman moralists. Already in the third century, Lactantius chided the Stoics for their restrictive and one-sided view of the passions. They call "mercy, desire, and fear diseases of the soul" *(morbos animi).*[6] Desire and fear are, of course, two of the cardinal passions, and mercy (which is not) is mentioned by Lactantius because of its place in the Scriptures. "Blessed are the merciful for they shall receive mercy *(misericordiam)*" (Matt. 5:7). Even though Lactantius offers an Aristotelian defense of the passions against the Stoics, the presence in the Bible of affections such as fear, desire, sorrow, gratitude, zeal, love, and, of course, compassion or mercy prompted him, as well as other Christian moralists, to rethink conventional assumptions. Though the issues were ancient, Christians came to them with new ideas and language and, in time, a new perspective. The end toward which one aspired was no longer seen as a life of virtue, wisdom, or possession of the "good" but fellowship with God or divinization. When Tertullian wrote a treatise "on patience," a virtue found in the Scriptures but ignored by Latin moralists, he did something similar. He made God rather than

---

ime, d'après les *Quaestiones ad Thalassium*," in *Maximus Confessor,* Actes du Symposium sur Maxime le Confesseur, Fribourg, 2-5 September 1980, ed. F. Heinzer and C. Schoenborn (Fribourg, 1982), 273-284.

5. For a survey of ancient views of the affections, see H. M. Gardiner, et al., *Feeling and Emotion: A History of Theories* (Westport, 1970), 58-118.

6. Text in *Divinae Institutiones* 6.14-17.

the sage the model of virtue. "God himself," he said, "was the example of patience."[7]

The Stoics, writes Lactantius, take away from us all the "affections by the impulse of which the soul is *moved.*" As Lactantius knew well, the term "moved" came from Aristotle. In the *De Motu Animalium,* when discussing the movement of the soul, Aristotle had argued that all movement can be reduced to "thought" and "desire."[8] Without a conception of what is to be done, we do not know what it is we are to do, but without desire, something that draws us to the object and keeps our sights fixed firmly on it, there is no possibility of movement. "The proximate reason for *movement,*" writes Aristotle, "is desire."[9] Drawing on Aristotle's explanation of human action, Lactantius argued that the Stoics "deprive human beings of all the affections by whose instigation the soul is *moved,* namely desire, delight, fear, grief." These affections, he continues, have been implanted in us by God for a reason; without them it is impossible to have a moral life. His statement "Without anger there can be no virtue,"[10] though not the most felicitous, makes the point. Anger, when properly used, can contribute to the virtuous life. If there is no movement toward the good (or away from evil) there can be no virtue.

For the Stoics, the goal of the sage was to be completely free of the passions, to reach a state of *apatheia.* Virtue required detachment from the unpredictable and disordered feelings that drive us.[11] Of course, some Christian thinkers, unlike Lactantius, found Stoic ethics congenial and sought to give the goal of *apatheia* a place in

7. Tertullian, *De Patientia* 2.1.

8. Martha Nussbaum, ed., *Aristotle's "De Motu Animalium"* (Princeton, 1978). See *De Motu Animalium* 700b18-19, 38-39.

9. Aristotle, *De Motu Animalium* 701a35.

10. *Div. Inst.* 6.15.

11. On this point see Martha Nussbaum's thorough and insightful article, "The Stoics on the Extirpation of the Passions," *Apeiron* 20 (1987): 129-177.

Christian life. Clement of Alexandria, for example, thought that *apatheia* was supported by the Scriptures. Although he recognized that there is a necessary role for the passions (perhaps better, appetites or instincts) in human life, for example, the desire for food, he refused to allow them any place in the moral life. The reason is that Christ lived a life free of the passions, and "after the Resurrection, the disciples learned to live in an unwavering disposition of self-discipline."[12] It is incumbent on the one who seeks perfection, that is, the true gnostic, to follow the example of Jesus and the apostles. The gnostic must be free "of all passion of the soul. For knowledge leads to discipline, discipline to habit and character which issues finally in a state of *apatheia*, not *metropotheia* (moderation of the passions)," as Clement pointedly remarks. "The fruit that comes from complete elimination of desire is *apatheia*."[13] The gnostic, like the apostles, he concludes, does not share even in those passions that are considered good, for example, delight, grief, and fear.[14]

These sentiments would have a powerful impact on Christian thinking during the next several centuries, especially after the rise of monasticism. The key figure here is of course Evagrius Ponticus. Because his approach to the religious life was at once theoretical as well as practical, his influence on later Christian thinkers, including Maximus, was great.[15] Evagrius believed that

12. Maximus took a quite different point of view. He said that the Logos had "not only become a full human being but also a human being fully subject to passion" (*PG* 91.1041d).

13. Clement, *Stromateis* 6.9.71, 74.

14. Clement, however, distinguishes *epithumia*, desire as an unwelcome passion, and *orexis*, a rational or well-ordered desire, and he recognizes the need for the latter in the life of virtue (*Stromateis* 3.11.71). On this point see David G. Hunter, "The Language of Desire: Clement of Alexandria's Transformation of Ascetic Discourse," in *Discursive Strategies, Ascetic Piety, and the Interpretation of Religious Literature, Semeia* 57 (Atlanta, 1992): 95-111.

15. On the influence of Evagrius on Maximus, see Marcel Viller, "Aux sources

the chief impediments to spiritual growth were "thoughts" *(logismoi)* that enter the soul and distract it from contemplating God. For Evagrius these thoughts are closely associated with the "passions," chiefly desire and anger, but also the other passions that create images of sensible objects. Through the senses, but also through memory (of things formerly known through the senses), the demons make an impression on the ruling principle, the mind. Only if one is able to silence the thoughts and fantasies that turn the soul away from its proper destiny can one achieve *apatheia.* "Those who are no longer susceptible to such thoughts are pure and free of passion *(apatheis).*"[16] As support for his views, Evagrius cited the words of the Psalmist: "Refrain from anger and forsake wrath" (Ps. 38:8).[17] For Evagrius the passions are "contrary to nature" and must be eradicated to free the mind from the domination of distracting images.[18]

An alternative view, closer to that of Lactantius, can be found in Gregory of Nyssa. Prior to Maximus he was the most influential critic of the Stoic view of the affections, at least in the East. Augustine, as we shall see, was also critical of the Stoics on this point. In his treatise *De Anima et Resurrectione,* Gregory asks: Are the passions (desire and fear) intrinsic to the soul? That is, are they part of human nature given at creation? Gregory argues that the passions are not "consubstantial with [human] nature."[19] Moses, for example, was a holy man of God who was successful in overcoming anger and desire. Yet Gregory is uneasy with the view that the affections must simply be overcome, and as his argument moves

---

de la spiritualité de saint Maxime: Les oeuvres d'Évagre le Pontique," *Revue d'ascétique et de mystique* 11 (1930): 156-184, 239-268, 331-336.

16. Evagrius, *PG* 79.1204d.

17. Evagrius, *PG* 79.1205c-d. Cf. Lam. 11:10 and 1 Tim. 2:8.

18. On this point see Elizabeth Clark, *The Origenist Controversy* (Princeton, 1993), 76-77.

19. Gregory of Nyssa, *Anim. Res.* (*PG* 46.50d).

forward he shows that they can be useful for acquiring virtue. "In their pursuit of the good the virtuous receive not a little assistance from these affections."[20] For example, Daniel's "desire" (which probably means his zeal in serving God alone) was praised (Dan. 10:12), and Phineas's "anger" pleased God (Num. 25:11). Further, the Scriptures say that "fear" is the beginning of wisdom (Prov. 9:10) and "godly grief" leads to salvation. The Bible teaches us "not simply to consider such things as harmful passions, for if so, the passions would not have been included among things which are helpful in achieving virtue."[21]

Gregory's scriptural support for his argument is bafflingly sketchy, especially when one recalls the many texts that could have been cited in support, for example, Psalm 42, "As the hart longs for living waters, so yearns my soul for you O God," or Psalm 63, "O God, you are my God, I seek you, my soul thirsts for you, my flesh faints for you, as in a dry and weary land where there is no water." But his point is clear. According to the Scriptures, the passions aided God's saints in their pursuit of virtue. Anger, fear, desire, and other passions are "instruments of the soul" given for the purpose of helping humans "choose good and evil." If they are directed to a good end they can be instruments of virtue, but if directed to an evil end they become instruments of vice. Fear, for example, can lead to obedience, and "the impulse of desire secures delight that is divine and unalloyed."[22]

Yet Gregory remains somewhat uneasy with the term "desire," for it carries negative (as well as positive) overtones in the Scriptures. Hence he proposes a distinction between desire and love (which of course in his vocabulary is a form of desire). Returning to his original statement that the passions were not part of human nature,

20. Gregory, *Anim. Res.* (*PG* 48.56c-57d).
21. Gregory, *Anim. Res.* (*PG* 48.57a).
22. Gregory, *Anim. Res.* (*PG* 48.61b).

he says that there will come a time when the "desiring principle" (sometimes called the concupiscible principle) will no longer exist. But if that is so, nothing will remain "to bring about movement" and to arouse a "yearning for the good." Even when one goes beyond desire and "exists wholly in the beautiful," there must be something that binds one to the good, and that, in the language of the Scriptures, is the "disposition to love." For love is nothing else than a "deep-seated relation to that which is pleasing." In the end, the soul, leaving behind desire, "clings to [the good] and mingles with it, through the movement and activity of love, fashioning itself to that which is being grasped continually and discovered." Hence Paul writes, "Love never ceases."[23]

Gregory, like Lactantius, retains the Aristotelian framework, that action requires movement as well as thought, and that movement is only possible with desire. But he goes beyond Lactantius (and Aristotle) by interpreting desire as love.[24] For Lactantius the affections were active in avoiding evil and pursuing good; Gregory, however, is more interested in the affections as a way of establishing and maintaining the relation to God. Hence he replaces "desire" by "love," which opens the way for a fuller appropriation of the biblical understanding of love, for example, "You shall *love* the Lord your God with all your heart and with all your soul and with all your might."

Which brings me to Maximus.[25] In the introduction to the *Quaestiones ad Thalassium,* Maximus makes clear that the passions (or affections) are central to the work. Here are a few of the topics

23. Gregory, *Anim. Res.* (*PG* 48.89a).

24. To speak of desire and love in relation to God was of course not unique to Christian thinkers. Similar conceptions appear in Greek thinkers, for example Plotinus. See René Arnou, *Le Désir de Dieu dans la Philosophie de Plotin* (Rome, 1967).

25. For a fuller account of the history of Christian interpretation of the passions, one would have to consider Nemesius of Emesa, who dealt with the topic at length. See *Nat. hom.* 16-21.

he promises to consider: How many passions are there and of what kind? What is their origin? To what end does each aspire? In which faculty of the soul or which member of the body are they implanted? What is the meaning of the name given to each passion and its abilities? What are their hidden machinations and plots? How do some surreptitiously enter in for apparently good reasons? How do they retreat, feint? What creates their subtlety, their pettiness, their enmity, their self-importance, their obstinacy, and their persistence? What is the state of the soul when it is receptive to various kinds of demons? What is the manner of their presence in us, and of the great diversity and variety of the phantasies they produce in our dreams while we sleep? Are they confined to a certain part of the soul or the body or to the soul or the body as a whole?[26]

On the basis of this passage in which the passions seem to be presented chiefly as vices (at one point he identifies them with the activity of demons), one would think that Maximus's chief effort in the *Ad Thalassium* is to set forth the many ways in which the passions hinder genuine spiritual growth.[27] And there is much in the book that lends support to this view.[28] Yet when one turns to the first question in the book he surprises us by emphasizing not the evil that the passions work but the good that they make possible. He asks: "Are the passions evil in themselves or do they

26. *Quaest. Thal.*, prol., p. 23, lns. 108ff.

27. Maximus had read Evagrius. In the chapters on love he writes: "Some of the passions are of the body, some of the soul. Those of the body take their origin in the body; those of the soul from exterior things. Love and self-control cut away both of them, the former those of the soul, the latter those of the body." The same ideas are found in similar terms in Evagrius's *Praktikos,* chap. 35.

28. *Quaest. Thal.* 34, p. 235, lns. 20-21. Contending with the passions is a key element of the kind of literature of which the *Quaestiones ad Thalassium* is a part. See Paul M. Blowers, *Exegesis and Spiritual Pedagogy in Maximus the Confessor: An Investigation of the "Quaestiones ad Thalassium"* (Notre Dame, 1991), 13, 38, 46.

become evil from the way that they are used?" Appealing to Gregory of Nyssa, he answers that the passions were not part of the original creation of human beings.[29] This would seem to imply that the passions are intrinsically evil, the result of the fall, but instead he stresses the positive role they play in the spiritual life. "In the devout the passions become good when, prudently turning away from the things of the body, they concern themselves with the possession of heavenly things. For example, *desire* brings about an insatiable movement of spiritual longing for divine things, *delight* a quiet enjoyment of the activity of the mind as it is enticed by the divine gifts, *fear* unceasing diligence to avoid sin in light of the future punishment, and *distress* a scrupulous fixation on present evil. . . ." Without the passions, he continues, human beings would be unable "to hold fast to virtue and knowledge" and would have only an impetuous and ephemeral attachment to the good. As biblical warrant for his view he cites 1 Corinthians 10:5, where Paul's "thoughts" are understood to refer to the passions. "All these things are good when they are used by those who subject every thought [passion] to the obedience of Christ."

Note first that Maximus explicitly mentions the four cardinal passions and that he interprets them in a thoroughly classical way. By his choice of terms, for example, "insatiable movement" for desire and "quiet enjoyment" for delight, he allows the reader to see that there is an internal logic to the four cardinal passions. The choice of four is not arbitrary. Just as the ancient moralists spoke of four cardinal virtues — prudence, justice, courage, and temperance — so they also spoke of four cardinal passions, desire, delight, fear, and distress. In classical moral philosophy the classification of the four passions turned on two axes, a distinction

29. Gregory, *De virg.* 12.2.4-11. See also Evagrius, *Divers. malig.* 2.29 (*PG* 79.1201c).

between good and bad, and a distinction between that which one possesses and that which one yearns to possess.[30] Maximus speaks of two movements, one a movement toward the good and the other a movement away from evil (desire and fear relate to that which is expected),[31] and two possessions, one suffering evil, the other enjoying the good, or in Maximus's language, grief or delight over what is present, that is, what one possesses. The scheme, then, is intended to be comprehensive and will serve as a framework in which to present the particulars of the ascetic life, a movement *away* from evil and *toward* God, the goal of which is the *possession* of God, that is, delight in God.[32]

Second, in spite of his statement that the passions were not part of the original creation, his final comment qualifies that assertion. Everything depends on their "use," says Maximus. Parenthetically it might be noted that Augustine came to the same conclusion about the nature of the passions. "If their love is right, these affections [he mentions the four cardinal passions] are right in them."[33] The passions are not "blameworthy" (not subject to praise or blame in and of themselves) but are the "inseparable accompaniments of natural inclinations." For example, just as hunger and thirst have a necessary role in sustaining human life, so also are the passions "necessary for the acquiring of virtue."[34] It is possible, says Maximus, to speak of the "right use of our natural faculties."[35]

---

30. See Nussbaum, "The Stoics on the Extirpation of the Passions," 177.

31. *Nicomachean Ethics* 1104b9-12. Hence "moral virtue is the quality of acting in the best way in relation to pleasures and pains, and . . . vice is the opposite" (27-29).

32. Aristotle speaks of an "object of pursuit *(diokton)* and avoidance *(pseukton)* (*Motu Anim.* 701b33). Maximus uses the Aristotelian term *pseugo* in *Quaest. Thal.* 55, p. 489, ln. 135.

33. Augustine, *De civitate Dei* 14.9.

34. *Quaest. Thal.* 55, p. 489, lns. 233-234.

35. *PG* 91.1079b-d.

For Maximus the passions are evidence that human beings were created with an innate capacity, a natural faculty in the soul, to delight in spiritual things. When God made human nature "he did not create with it sensual pleasure or grief (i.e., the passions), but there was built into human beings a certain capacity for spiritual delight, by which, in an ineffable way, human beings would be able to enjoy God." The first human being, however, was moved by sensual things so that there "worked in him a delight that was sensual." Providentially, God set "grief" as a kind of opposition to delight. In other words, it was the abuse of the passions, not their existence, that led to the present lot of human beings. From the beginning, however, human nature had a capacity for delight in God. As Maximus puts it elsewhere, "Nothing that is natural and has been made by God is evil" (Maximus's word is "impure").[36]

The affections, then, are necessary for the virtuous life. Maximus, however, wants to say more. In the response to the first question of the *Ad Thalassium*, he says that the passions allow human beings to avoid evil so that they might "possess and hold fast to virtue *and* knowledge." In the passage cited above, where Maximus makes a similar point, he only mentions "virtue" *(arete)*, but here, significantly, he adds "knowledge" *(gnosis)*.[37] In this context knowledge means knowledge of God, and for Maximus knowledge of God does not simply mean knowing something; rather, it is knowledge that fashions the knower by that which is known. Such knowledge is not possible from a distance; it entails a relation. Hence it cannot be attained without the affection, that is, love, that binds the knower to the object of love. He writes: "Knowledge of divine things *without passion* does not persuade

36. *Quaest. Thal.* 27, pp. 201, lns. 163-165.
37. The conjunction of "virtue" and "knowledge" is very frequent in Maximus.

the mind to disdain material things completely, but rather resembles the mere thought of a thing of sense. . . . Just as the simple thought of human realities does not oblige the mind to disdain the divine, so neither does the simple knowledge of divine things persuade it fully to disdain human things. . . . Hence there is a need for the blessed *passion of holy love* which binds the mind to spiritual realities and persuades it to prefer the immaterial to the material and intelligible and divine things to those of sense."[38]

In conceiving of knowledge of God as participation and union with God, Maximus draws of course on the Holy Scriptures. In his commentary on the Gospel of John, Origen explained how the term "knowledge" is used in the Bible. He is commenting on John 8:19: "You know neither me nor my Father. If you knew me, you would know my Father also." "One should take note," he says, "that the Scripture says that those who are united to something or participate in something are said to know that to which they are united or in which they participate. Before such union and fellowship, even if they understand the reasons given for something, they do not know it." As illustration he mentions the union between Adam and Eve, which the Bible described as "Adam knew his wife Eve," and in 1 Corinthians 6:16-17, union with a prostitute. This shows, he says, that "knowing" means "being joined to" or "united with."[39]

In his discussion of the "use" of the passions in the spiritual life, then, it is significant that Maximus slips in the word "knowledge" alongside "virtue." By yoking the passions to knowledge and not simply to the attainment of virtue, Maximus provides a theoretical framework that makes a place for love. When knowledge is understood as participation and fellowship, love is its

38. Maximus, *Cent. car.* 3.66-67.
39. Origen, *Comm. in Joan.* 8:19; 19.4.21-25.

natural accompaniment.[40] In this Maximus shows a genuine affinity with Augustine's understanding of knowledge and love. As Bernard McGinn observes: "Love and knowledge are intertwined in Augustine's mystical consciousness."[41] More specifically, there are parallels in the way the two thinkers treat the passions and the virtues. I have already cited a passage on the passions, but Augustine and Maximus make similar statements about the virtues. Maximus writes: "All these [the four cardinal virtues] are brought together in the most noble virtue of all, I mean love."[42] Likewise, Augustine interprets the cardinal virtues as forms of the love of God. Temperance is "love keeping itself entire . . . for God; fortitude is love bearing everything for the sake of God; justice is love serving God alone, . . . and prudence is love making a right distinction between what helps it towards God and what hinders it."[43]

In Augustine as well as in Maximus, love is of course a form of desire. In the Scriptures, however, "desire" often carries negative overtones. For example, Paul exhorts the Thessalonians to learn how to "control" their bodies "in holiness and honor, not in the passion of desire" (1 Thess. 4:5). Hence there was some reluctance, as in Gregory, to use the term "desire" without qualification. "Love" was a far preferable term, because it is thoroughly biblical and its field of meaning is broader. Maximus uses both terms in tandem, allowing each one to color the meaning of the other. He writes: "For the mind of the one who is continually with God even his desire *(epithumia)* abounds beyond measure into a divine eros *(erota)* and whose entire irascible element is

---

40. On love and union, see *Quaest. Thal.* 54, p. 451, lns. 155-157.

41. Bernard McGinn, *The Foundations of Mysticism* (New York, 1992), 1:235.

42. Maximus, *PG* 91.1249b. Also: "The end *(telos)* of the virtues is love" (*Quaest. Thal.* 54, p. 451, ln. 155).

43. Augustine, *Mor. ecc. cat.* 15.25.

transformed into divine love *(agape)*. For by an enduring participation in the divine illumination it has become altogether shining
bright, and having bound its passible element to itself it . . .
turned it around to a never ending eros *(erota)*, completely chang-
ing over from earthly things to divine."[44]

Here, as always, Maximus is scrupulous in his choice of
terms. By using "desire" and "love" in connection with *eros*, he
provides an interpretation of the passion "desire" in light of the
biblical term for "love" *(agape)*, while at the same time filling the
biblical term with the echoes that are heard in "desire." Of course
the term *eros*, which is not used in the New Testament, and seldom
in the Old, provides the link. It is a shrewd move and one that
Maximus may have learned from Pseudo-Dionysius the
Areopagite. In what seems a deliberately playful passage, Pseudo-
Dionysius explains how the language of love works in the Scripture. "Do not think," he says, "that in giving status to the term
'yearning' *(eros)* I am running counter to scripture." For example,
what does one make of this passage from Proverbs about Wisdom
(which for Dionysius was Christ): "Desire her and she shall hold
you; exalt her and she will extol you" (Prov. 4:6). The careful
reader of the Bible will discover, he continues, that in certain
places the Scriptures use the term *agape* when they mean desire
or erotic love, implying that this is the case in other passages. His
example comes from the Septuagint version of 1 Samuel chapter
1, David's lament over Jonathan, at the end of which he speaks
of the love between them. David cries out: "Your love for me was

---

44. *Cent. car.* 2.48. Elsewhere he says that after breaking away from earthly
things the mind "finally transfers its whole longing *(pothos)* to God" (*Cent. car.*
3.72); also, "the faculty of desire in which the divine love consists, and through
which it readily affixes itself with desire to the pure godhead, has an unwavering
longing for that which is desired. There is also the irascible faculty, by which it
binds itself tightly to the divine peace and draws up the movement of desire to
divine love" (*Quaest. Thal.* 49, p. 355, lns. 75-81).

greater than love for women." Here where one would expect to find the term *eros* the Scriptures use *agapesis*. From which Dionysius concludes: "To those listening properly to the divine things the term *love* is used by the sacred writers in divine revelation with the exact same meaning as the term *eros*."[45]

In the scheme of the passions, the two concupiscible passions are desire and delight. Desire, as we have seen, is transformed into the biblical love; similarly Maximus reinterprets pleasure or delight in what is possessed with the help of another biblical term, "joy." He writes: "Without virtue and knowledge [note the conjunction] it is impossible to obtain salvation. For those who are wholly devoted to God . . . the irrational powers of the soul" are tamed and "assimilated." This means that "anger and desire are transformed, the one into love, the other into joy. For what is proper to joy is leaping about in a way befitting God, as great John, the forerunner and herald of the truth, leaped in his mother's womb (Luke 1:41) or David king of Israel [danced with abandon] when the ark was given a resting place [in Jerusalem]." In these two instances, John leaping in the womb of Elizabeth when she heard Mary's greetings and David dancing when the ark had found its resting place in Jerusalem, desire and longing had given way to delight, to the enjoyment of that which previously had been a matter of longing.

Maximus, like other Christian writers, is more interested in the positive passions, that is, desire and delight, than in the negative passions, fear and grief. The reason for this is that his approach to the passions is primarily theological, not moral. The goal of the Christian life is not simply to displace evil and attain virtue, but it is to possess that which alone can bring delight, the one true God. Even anger's intensity is transformed by Maximus into a concupiscible affection. "Our reason also should therefore

45. Pseudo-Dionysius, *Div. nom.* 11-12.

be moved to seek God, the force of desire should struggle to possess him, and that of anger to hold on to him, or rather, to speak more properly, the whole mind should tend to God, stretched out as a sinew by the temper of anger, and burning with longing for the highest reaches of desire."[46]

Of course, for Maximus, as for Gregory of Nyssa, perfection is never a simple coming to rest, a standing still. Maximus, who loved paradoxical phrases, spoke of "ever-moving repose" or "stationary movement," by which he meant that the soul that loves God is at once at rest in God and at the same time in perpetual motion drawn toward God. "All things created according to time," he writes, "become perfect when they cease their natural growth. But everything that the knowledge of God effects according to virtue, when it reaches perfection, moves to further growth. For the end of the latter becomes the beginning of the former. Indeed, the one who by practicing the virtues keeps in check the substance of past things begins other, more divine patterns. For God never ceases from good things, just as there was no beginning of good things."[47]

One comes away from reading Maximus, as one does in reading Augustine, with the sense that the old vessels found in the classical moral tradition have difficulty containing the new wine. Indeed Maximus's thinking on the affections moves along a path that is not unlike that of Augustine. Consider, for example, in light of Maximus's discussion of perpetual growth, a passage from Augustine's commentary on the First Epistle of John, in which he describes the soul as a leather bag that stretches to make room for God. "The whole life of a good Christian," he writes, "is a holy desire. However, that which you desire you do not yet

---

46. Maximus, *Or. dom.* (*PG* 896c); ET in *Maximus Confessor: Selected Writings*, trans. George C. Berthold (New York, 1985), 113.

47. Maximus, *Cap. theol.* 1.35 (*PG* 90.1096c), in Berthold, *Maximus Confessor*, 134-135 (slightly revised).

see; but by desiring you become capable of being filled by that which you will see when it comes. For just as in filling a leather bag . . . one stretches the skin . . . and by stretching one makes it capable of holding more; so God by deferring that for which we long, stretches our desire; by increasing desiring stretches the mind; by being stretched, it becomes more capable of being filled."[48] Other Augustinian themes, the virtues as forms of love, the conjunction of love and knowledge, "cleaving to God" (expressed in his use of Psalm 73, "for me to cleave to God is good"), and the notion of "enjoying God," also have parallels in Maximus. Von Balthasar speculates about the possibility of "contact" with Augustinian ideas during Maximus's long stay in North Africa, but he concludes, rightly, that Maximus is much too original for such an interpretation. "Maximus speaks less as one who has learned something from someone else, than as one who is in full control of what is distinctively his own."[49]

That is surely true. Yet it is perhaps more to the point, at least on the topic of the affections, to underscore Maximus's affinity with other Christian thinkers rather than his originality. The direction he pursued was set already in the third century by Lactantius (and before him by the Scriptures) and explored in depth by Gregory of Nyssa and Nemesius of Emesa, and of course by Augustine. In later centuries thinkers in both East and West, including John of Damascus, Gregory Palamas, and Thomas Aquinas, built on these foundations.[50] Which returns me to Jonathan Edwards. Whatever the differences between Edwards and Maximus, in vocation, in theological outlook, in style of argument, and in temperament, it is not insignificant that an American, a child of the Reformation, a Calvinist, a revivalist, a

48. Augustine, *Trac. in Epist. Joann.* 4.6 (*Patrologia Latina* 35.2008-2009).

49. Von Balthasar, *Kosmische Liturgie,* 408-409.

50. See Mark D. Jordan, "Aquinas's Construction of a Moral Account of the Passions," *Freiburger Zeitschrift für Philosophie und Theologie* 33 (1986): 71-97.

pastor — not an ascetic — discerned the essential point, that the religion of the Bible places religion "very much in the affections" and has nothing to do with a "state of indifference." On the matter of the affections Christian thinkers transcended divisions we take for granted, the differences between East and West, ancient and modern, Catholic and Protestant, monastic and lay. Ancient asceticism, at least as we come to know it in Maximus the Confessor, is perennial. What ascetics saw, others saw; and what they saw was not only for ascetics.

8

Memory and the
Christian Intellectual Life

I T IS EASY to get religion, something else to hold onto it. As in dieting, many find it easy to take off weight, but quite another matter to keep it off. Religion, however, unlike dieting, is not a solitary business. Unless one is an unchastened Jamesian, religion is communal, and for religious men and women, the challenge is not only to keep the faith for ourselves but also to hand it on to the next generation. Only with difficulty and imagination can we transmit our experiences to those after us who feel, think, and act differently than we do. For the task of handing on the faith, the warm heart is insufficient, as the parent who is "born again" or "converted" soon realizes when facing the task of giving his or her children religious instruction.

To be sure, without affections there can be no religious life, as we learn from thinkers as diverse as Augustine of Hippo, Maximus the Confessor, and Jonathan Edwards. Affective lan-

Originally published in *Reasoned Faith*, ed. Frank F. Birtel (New York, 1993), 141-155. Reprinted by permission of Crossroad Publishing Co.

guage permeates the Bible."[1] With the development of early Christian thought, the vocabulary of the spiritual life expanded so that words such as *love, desire,* and *longing* became as familiar as *faith, obedience,* and *knowledge.* The rich imagery of the Bible — for example, "As the deer longs for flowing streams, so longs my soul for you, O God" (Ps. 42) — was complemented by the passionate love of the saints — for example, "My love of you, O Lord, is not some vague feeling: it is positive and certain. Your word struck into my heart and from that moment I loved you" (Augustine).[2]

Although there can be no faith without the affections, in a culture steeped in the jargon of psychology the subtle role of the affections in Christian life is too readily supplanted by a shriveled and subjective notion of faith. Indeed, so often is the term *faith* used to refer solely to the act of believing that in popular speech the object of faith seems irrelevant, as though it is the believing that counts, not what one believes. Faith, in this view, is self-legitimizing, impervious to examination, correction, or argument, and has its home in the private imaginings of the believer or in the sheltered world of religious communities. In the same way, the term *value* is used without reference to the good, as though all values are of equal worth and equal validity.

It is quite possible, however, as our daily experience teaches, to put faith in things that are illusory or false. Faith is only as good as its object; if the object of our faith is trustworthy, then it is reasonable to put our trust in it. If not, then it does not deserve our trust. Credulity is no virtue. A necessary component of faith is reason. The phrase *reasonable faith* was first used in the fourth century by Hilary of Poitiers, sometimes called the Latin

1. See John Burnaly, *Amor Dei: A Study of the Religion of St. Augustine* (London, 1938).
2. Augustine, *Confessions* 10.6.

Athanasius because of his defense of the doctrine of the Trinity. He believed that "Faith is akin to reason and accepts its aid." When the mind lays hold of God in faith, it knows that it can "rest with assurance, as on some peaceful watch-tower."[3] There is no leap of faith into the unknown for Hilary. In his view as in the view of all early Christian thinkers, faith was not a subjective attitude or feeling but a reasoned conviction. Whether speaking about faith in human beings or belief in God, the church fathers knew that faith cannot be self-authenticating and that to believe in something false or ignoble is not admirable, but foolish, like trusting a person who is an incorrigible liar.

Even a cursory study of the history of Christian thought will show that the charge of fideism caricatures the Christian intellectual tradition. Yet this caricature has become part of the way we tell the story of Western culture. From Edward Gibbon in the eighteenth century to historians of the present, Christianity has been charged with substituting authority and uncritical faith for reason, philosophy, and science. In the eighteenth century the encyclopedist Marquis de Condorcet wrote: "Contempt for the humanities was one of the principal characteristics of Christianity. It had to avenge itself against the insults offered by philosophy. . . . Christianity feared that spirit of investigation and doubt, that confidence in one's own reason, which is the scourge of all religious beliefs. . . . The triumph of Christianity was the signal for the complete decay of the sciences and philosophy."[4]

No doubt one of the reasons why faith has been divorced from reason is that, by laying stress on the attitude of the believer rather than on the truth of the thing believed, it is easier for people to negotiate our diverse and heterogeneous society. That

3. Hilary of Poitiers, *De Trinitate* 1.8.
4. Cited in Peter Gay, *The Enlightenment, An Interpretation: The Rise of Modern Paganism* (New York, 1966), 212.

attitude is also thought to discourage religious warfare. If faith is an affair of the believing subject and is self-authenticating, then it is easier for us to tolerate differences and live together in peace and harmony. A genial pluralism offers a protected place for individuals and communities of whatever religious belief to practice their faith without external hindrance.

Yet this form of religious peace has a price, for by acquiescing in a subjective notion of faith, religious people unwittingly empty faith of its cognitive character. When the object of faith becomes secondary to the act of believing, theology becomes reflection on faith, not reasoned speech about God. The theological enterprise may be variously useful or frivolous depending on one's point of view, but it makes no cognitive claims. It is valuable chiefly as an instrument to nurture the identity of a particular community. Hence, theology can only speak about meaning "for us" or "for them," that is, whatever works in a particular community, and can make no claim to speak about what is true. This is, of course, a reversal of the classical Christian (and Jewish) view that theology's object is God. Once the object of faith is abandoned, theology's object inevitably becomes human experience. Similarly, when talk of the good gives way to the language of values, we inevitably abandon the notion that some values are better than others, and that the *summum bonum* orders all lesser values.

But it is not my purpose here to elaborate on faith and reason, or on the question of values, at least not in the narrow sense of those terms. I begin with these observations because I want to discuss tradition.

The church is a living community that is the bearer of ancient traditions received from those who have gone before. In the marketplace of ideas, however, particular commitments, that is, traditions, are thought to be limiting and restrictive because they rest on authority and exalt the wisdom of the past over supposed rational insights of the present. Enlightenment thinkers, writes Alasdair MacIntyre, hoped that "reason would displace authority and tradition. Rational justification was to appeal to principles undeniable by any rational person and therefore independent of all those social and cultural particularities which the Enlightenment thinkers took to be mere accidental clothing of reason in particular times and places."[5]

So deeply have these ideas penetrated into our consciousness that even religious thinkers have taken them as axiomatic. The mark of rationality, it is assumed, is autonomy. Unless a thinker is freed from the constraints of inherited beliefs and institutions, he or she cannot engage in the spirit of free inquiry that leads to truth. Only if the scholar frees himself from the claims of tradition and becomes independent of external constraints (i.e., tradition) can he properly carry out his work of research, scholarship, and original thinking.

"The traditional Christian theologian," writes David Tracy, "of whatever tradition, preached and practiced a morality of belief in and obedience to the tradition and a fundamental loyalty to the church-community's beliefs. The modern historian and scientist — whether in natural or social sciences — preaches and practices an exactly contrary morality. For him, one cannot investigate a cognitive claim with integrity if one insists simultaneously that the claim is believable because tradition has believed." Tracy applies these same principles to the theologian: "The fundamental ethical commitment of the theologian qua theologian remains to that community of scientific inquiry whose province logically includes whatever issue is under investigation." In Tracy's view, the theologian must be committed to the "ethical model of the autonomous inquirer."[6]

5. Alasdair MacIntyre, *Whose Justice? Which Rationality?* (Notre Dame, Ind., 1988), 6.

6. David Tracy, *Blessed Rage for Order: The New Pluralism in Theology* (New York, 1975), 6-7.

Now there is something to what Tracy and others like him say. As early as Origen of Alexandria, Christian thinkers claimed that their ideas should be judged by the "common notions" that are at work within the intellectual community. The openness of Christian thinkers in the last two hundred years to modern thinking is a remarkable sign of confidence in reason as well as in the Christian tradition. They believed, rightly, that truth was one and that if one joined with others in the quest for truth, the results could only be beneficial for Christianity. Christian thought has always been a critical and rational enterprise, and at its best has welcomed the wisdom of the world into the household of faith.

Nevertheless, Christian thinkers have also known that they were bearers of a tradition. "That which I have received, I have handed on to you," wrote Saint Paul (1 Cor. 15:3). This tradition, exhibited first in the Scriptures, was later subjected to critical examination, tested in the lives of countless men and women, defended against its critics, and elaborated in myriad social and cultural settings. Hence I am a bit baffled why one should assume, as Tracy apparently does, that reason is to be found only outside of tradition and that genuine rationality requires "autonomy." This premise seems to invite a willful amnesia, a self-imposed affliction that would rob our lives of depth and direction. Yet Tracy believes (or did when he wrote *Blessed Rage for Order*) that the liaison with tradition obstructs the path to enlightenment. To be an intellectual, in this view, is to loosen the moorings that bind one to a particular tradition or a living religious community.

That such ideas could take hold in the academy is evidence of how insular intellectuals can be, even religious ones. In many fields of creative work, immersion in tradition is the presupposition for excellence and originality. Think, for example, of music. On Saturday mornings, I often listen to a jazz show on National Public Radio that features interviews with famous and not-so-famous jazz pianists, saxophonists, drummers, trumpeters, etc., and I am regularly struck at how they speak with such respect of teachers and masters, and how to a person they learned to play the piano by first playing in someone else's style or learned to blow the trumpet by imitating Louis Armstrong or someone else. Similarly, one is impressed with how often a performer like folk singer Jean Redpath speaks about tradition as the necessary condition for making and singing folk music. How often we are admonished not to let the old traditions be forgotten. Why? Surely not for historical or archaeological reasons, but because musicians, like painters and writers and sculptors, know in their fingertips or vocal cords or ears that imitation is the way to excellence and originality.

Without tradition, learning is arduous at best, impossible at worst. In most things in life — learning to speak, making cabinets, playing the violin — the only way to learn is by imitation, by letting someone else guide our movements until we learn to do the thing on our own. I am not sure why this is so, but I suspect a chief reason is that only in the act of doing and participating do we truly know and understand. To do something well, we have to give ourselves over to it. T. S. Eliot made this point about literary criticism: "You don't really criticize any author to whom you have never surrendered yourself. . . . You have to give yourself up, and then recover yourself, and the third moment is having something to say, before you have wholly forgotten both surrender and recovery."[7]

Reason, it seems, is found within rather than outside of things; it is not an abstract quality that exists independently in the human mind — which means, of course, that it is *reasonable* to allow one's hands to be guided by a master, and foolish to go it alone, as though one could learn to play the violin or sculpt a statue by studying a set of instructions. In this context, the ideal of the autonomous individual is glaringly inappropriate, for we

7. Cited in Cleo McNelly Kearns, *T. S. Eliot and Indic Traditions* (Cambridge, 1987), 3.

recognize that here the true mark of rationality is to apprentice oneself to another rather than to strike out on one's own. To paraphrase Kenny Rogers, "There'll be time enough" for originality when the apprenticeship is done.

What applies to violin-playing or cabinet-making also applies, *mutatis mutandis,* to the intellectual life. The way we learn to think is by reading good thinkers and letting their thoughts form our thoughts. Matthew Arnold reminds us: "Commerce with the ancients appears to me to produce, in those who constantly practice it, a steadying and composing effect upon their judgment, not of literary works only, but of men and events in general. They are like persons who have had a very weighty and impressive experience; they are more truly than others under the empire of facts, and more independent of the language current among those with whom they live."[8]

From the ancients, we learn to use language in a precise way, to understand the inner logic of ideas, to discern the deeper relation between seemingly disparate concepts, to discriminate between things that appear similar, to know what is central and what is peripheral. And in the process we are tutored in humility, for we see that the things worthy of reception by us have been tested in the fire of human experience. As Charles M. Wood has pointed out, "Concepts . . . are creatures of history: they come into being, are molded and occasionally transformed through their complex and flexible relationships to other concepts and to the particularities of human existence, and may even fade and wither. The lives of concepts are inextricably related to the lives of actual persons and communities."[9] Hence

8. Matthew Arnold, "Preface to the First Edition of Poems (1853)," in *Poetry and Literary Criticism of Matthew Arnold,* by A. D. Culler (Boston, 1961), 212.

9. Charles Wood, *The Formation of Christian Understanding: An Essay in Theological Hermeneutics* (Philadelphia, 1981), 76.

there can be no genuine Christian intellectual life that is not rooted in history.

In the first volume of his *Systematic Theology,* Wolfhart Pannenberg observes that for a long time he had thought it possible to present theology in such a way that its chief themes could be divorced from the "bewildering multiplicity of historical questions." Only then could the systematic unity of Christian theology become evident. Contrary to his own expectations, however, he found that this way of presenting theology had to be discarded. He writes: "Christian teaching is of such a character that it is through and through a historical creation."[10] Its content rests on the historical person of Jesus Christ and on the historical interpretations that arose as a result of his life, death, and resurrection. The language of Christian thought cannot be extracted from its place in history, for without history, language loses particularity, and hence intelligibility.

The first question, then, that a Christian intellectual should ask is not "what should be believed?" or "what should one think?" but "*whom* should one trust?" Augustine understood this well, and in his early apologetic work, *On True Religion,* he links the appeal to reason with trust in the community and authority. Our notion of authority is so attenuated that it may be useful to look a bit more closely at what Augustine means by authority. For us, authority is linked to offices and institutions, to those who hold jurisdiction, hence to notions of power. We speak of submitting to authority or of obeying authority, and assume that authority has to do with the *will,* not with the *understanding.*

Yet there is another sense of authority that traces its source to the *auctor* in *auctoritas.* Sometimes translated "author," *auctor* can designate a magistrate, writer, witness, someone who is wor-

10. Wolfhart Pannenberg, *Systematische Theologie,* vol. 1 (Göttingen, 1988), 7.

thy of trust, a guarantor who attests to the truth of a statement, one who teaches or advises. Authority in this view has to do with trustworthiness, with the confidence a teacher earns through teaching with truthfulness, if you will. To say we need authority is much the same as saying we need teachers, or to use my earlier analogy, that we need to become apprentices.

Augustine expressed his idea of authority in *On True Religion* by saying: "Authority invites trust and prepares human beings for reason. Reason leads to understanding and knowledge. But reason is not entirely absent from authority, for we have got to consider whom we have to believe." In the Library of Christian Classics translation of this passage, the first words are rendered: "Authority demands belief."[11] Translated in this way, especially the term *demands,* the sentence is misleading. For Augustine is not thinking of an authority that *demands* or *commands* or *coerces* (terms that require an act of will), but of a truth that engenders confidence because of who tells it to us.

Authority resides in a person who by actions as well as words invites trust and confidence. Augustine's model for authority is the relation of a teacher to a student, a master to a disciple, not a magistrate to a subject. The student's trust is won not simply by words but also by actions, by the kind of person the teacher is — in short, by character. When Gregory Thaumaturgus, a young man from Asia Minor, went to Caesarea in Palestine to study with Origen, the greatest intellectual of his day, he said that he did so because he wanted to have "fellowship" with "that man."

Authority rests neither on external legitimization nor on power but on trustworthiness, or in Augustine's words, on truth. Its purpose is to clarify and illuminate, that is, to aid understanding, and its instrument is argument, not coercion. If a teacher is

11. Augustine, *De Vera Religione* xxiv.45 in *Augustine: Earlier Writings,* trans. John H. S. Burleigh, The Library of Christian Classics (Philadelphia, 1953), 247.

constantly saying "believe me" without giving reasons, the student may for a time assent, but he will not understand nor be convinced, and in time will stop listening. As Saint Thomas wrote, "If the teacher determines the question by appeal to authorities only, the student will be convinced that the thing is so, but will have acquired no knowledge or understanding, and he will go away with an empty mind."[12]

Thus far, I have spoken rather generally about the place of tradition in the intellectual life, but since I have made so much of particularity, it is time to be more specific. Apprenticeship is a purely formal category and, like reason, cannot be discussed in the abstract. Here the point about "whom shall we trust" becomes critical, for just as there are different styles of playing the piano, so there are different ways of thinking. What makes the difference between ways of thinking is not only the subject matter (whether law or biology or mathematics or statecraft or philosophy) but the sources that one draws on.

A particularly acute problem for Christian intellectuals today, especially those who work in philosophy, theology, and related fields, is that they have hired themselves out as apprentices to a body of literature that is drawn almost wholly from the nineteenth and twentieth centuries. For various reasons, we assume that the post-Enlightenment sources formulate the problems that are distinctive to our age, and hence make a unique claim on our attention. Other sources — the Bible, the writings of the church fathers, the treatises of the scholastics — belong to the past and to the domain of historians and biblical scholars.

Further, we assume that the task of the intellectual is to "translate" the substance of the tradition into contemporary language and categories. How, it is asked, are we to speak of God

12. Thomas Aquinas, *Quaestiones quodlibetales*, ed. P. Mandonnet (Paris, 1926), 155.

in an age of light bulbs and computers? The assumed answer is that we need to translate the idiom of the Scriptures into the idiom of our own time, to discuss the biblical faith in terms intelligible in the nonbiblical categories of today.

The difficulty with this program of translation is that the language of the Bible is irreplaceable, and more often than not the consequence of "translation" is that the language of the Scriptures is supplanted by another language or relegated to the footnotes. It ceases to be the vehicle of thought. As necessary as it is to "translate" the Bible into the thought patterns of our age, it is also the case that Christians in every generation must learn afresh how to think and imagine *in* the language and idiom of the Scriptures.

Let me illustrate the point with the trinitarian language of Father and Son. My example comes from the dispute between Gregory of Nyssa, the fourth-century bishop, theologian, and spiritual writer, and Eunomius, a second-generation Arian who believed that Christ was "unlike" the Father. Eunomius summed up his doctrine as follows: We believe in the "supreme and absolute being, and in another being existing by reason of the First (the Son), and a third being not ranking with either of these but inferior to the one as to its cause, to the other as to its energy." This was a rather startling argument for a Christian bishop, especially in light of the Council of Nicaea's confession (325 C.E.) that the Son was "of the same substance" as the Father.

Gregory, in response, appeals to the language of Scripture. He says that Eunomius "corrects as it were the expressions of the Gospel, and will not use the words . . . by which our Lord conveyed the mystery [of the Holy Trinity] to us; he suppresses the names of 'Father, Son, and Holy Spirit,' and speaks of a 'Supreme and absolute Being,' instead of the Father, of 'another existing through it, but after it' instead of the Son, and of a 'third ranking with neither of these two' instead of the Holy Spirit."

Now one might reply that Gregory, by simply appealing to the authority of Scripture and the words of Jesus, ignores the real issue: How is the language of Scripture to be understood by people who have been formed in a Hellenistic culture? What point is there in defending the metaphorical language of the Bible in the context of a genuine theological dispute about the relation of the Son to the Father, a dispute, moreover, that has arisen precisely *because* of the imprecision and diversity of the biblical language? Gregory, however, was as much aware of the difficulty as was Eunomius, and so he proceeded to give reasons why the biblical language has to be respected and cherished and used.

The words one uses, Gregory argues, make a difference; terms cannot be indiscriminately exchanged, as though the content of a proposition remains the same no matter what the vehicle. The term *Father*, for example, is quite different from "Supreme and absolute being," and Son from "one existing after the other," says Gregory, because when the words *Father* and *Son* are spoken, we recognize at once "the proper and natural relationship to one another" that the terms imply. These terms signify a relationship that the others do not. By abandoning the terms *Father* and *Son*, Eunomius does not simply jettison the biblical language; he also abandons "the idea of relationship which enters the ear with the words." Similarly, Eunomius' way of designating the Holy Spirit does not make clear that the Holy Spirit is a "distinct entity."[13]

I pick my illustration from Gregory of Nyssa because he is one of the most philosophical of all early Christian thinkers, a man who rigorously subjected the biblical tradition to critical analysis. Yet he also believed that the Scriptures had come from God and that the language of the Scriptures was not simply the result of historical

13. Gregory of Nyssa, *Contra Eunomium* 1.155-160, ed. Werner Jaeger (Leiden, 1960), 73-75. For English translation, see *Nicene and Post-Nicene Fathers*, Second Series (Grand Rapids, n.d.), 5:50-51.

accident or cultural conditioning. The Scriptures were a firm point of reference, rooted in the apostolic age, and there could be no genuine talk of God that ignored the biblical language. He approached the Scriptures with humility, looked to them for instruction, and believed that he was subject to them, not they to him.

The difficulty with the idea of "translating" biblical truth into nonbiblical language, as Janet Soskice observes in her fine book *Metaphor and Religious Language,* is that it assumes that "revelation exists as a body of free-floating truths." Meaning takes precedence over words, for what is essential, it is claimed, can be had independent of the language, the metaphors, the practices and form of life that have been the bearer of the meaning.[14]

Soskice illustrates her point by reference to the biblical metaphor of water: "Ho, every one who thirsts come to the water" (Isa. 55:1). She shows how this image runs throughout the Scriptures ("fountain of living waters" [Jer. 2:13]; "rivers of living waters" [John 7:37-38]) and Christian tradition (e.g., in the words of Teresa of Avila, who said: "I cannot find anything more apt for the explanation of certain spiritual things than this element of water; for, as I am ignorant and my wit gives me no help, and I am so fond of this element, I have looked at it more attentively than at other things").

The constant repetition of metaphor has gone hand-in-hand with typological interpretation of the Scriptures. To say that God is a "fountain of living water" or a fortress or vinekeeper or king, Soskice notes, "requires an account not merely of fountains, rocks, vines, and kings, but of a whole tradition of experiences and of the literary tradition which records and interprets them." The Christian imagination is biblical; for this reason, certain emblematic metaphors, ways of speaking, and events are given priority over others. Soskice writes, "The Old Testament's importance is not principally

14. Janet Martin Soskice, *Metaphor and Religious Language* (Oxford, 1985), 154.

as a set of propositions but as the milieu from which Christian belief arose and indeed still arises, for these books are the source of Christian descriptive language and particularly of metaphors which have embodied a people's understanding of God."[15] Further, the value of the biblical language is not only that it is biblical (that is to say, authoritative), but that it is grounded in the experience of men and women who have known the God about which it speaks.

Language is a vehicle of memory. Few things are more satisfying than to hear old and familiar words spoken or read anew to us. Like the madeleine cake in Proust's *A la recherche du temps perdu,* language not only makes alive (or makes present, to use a sacramental term) what gets lost in the recesses of the mind; it also molds our experience, stirs our imagination, holds before us the same things that were known by earlier generations, and keeps our mind trained on that to which the language refers, the God of Abraham, Isaac, Jacob, and Jesus. A pernicious feature of much historical criticism is that it unravels the cord linking the language of the Bible to the living God, and trains us to look away from the ostensible meaning to meanings that, however interesting, are not rooted in history or experience.

The Christian intellectual tradition, then, is inescapably historical. Without memory, our intellectual life is impoverished, barren, ephemeral, subject to the whims of the moment. Memory locates us in the corporate and the particular. There is no memory that is not rooted in communal experience — a strange fact that we all experience whenever we return to the place where we grew up and talk to family and friends, yet one that is often forgotten in abstract thought. Just as there can be no human life without the bricks and wood, the trees, hills, and rivers, the neighbors and family and friends that make up the world of each of us, so there can be no Christian intellectual life without reference to

15. Soskice, *Metaphor,* 159.

the writings of the prophets and evangelists, the doctrines of the church fathers, the conceptual niceties of the scholastics, the language of the liturgy, the songs of the poets and hymn writers, the exploits of the martyrs, and the holy tales of the saints.

The Christian intellectual is inescapably bound to those persons and ideas and events that have created the Christian memory, as Dante understood so well. Across the pages of the *Divine Comedy* stride an unparalleled cast of characters: Virgil and Beatrice, the Blessed Virgin, Saint Bernard, Potiphar's wife, Cato the Elder, King Solomon and Justinian, Pope Gregory the Great — whose views on angels Dionysius the Aeropagite corrected — popes Boniface VIII and John XXII, Saint John examining Dante on love, and Marco Lombardo discoursing on free will — characters presented not as a series of disconnected lives or philosophical ideas, but as part of a grand story held together by one thing: how every person and event and idea stands in relation to the "never ending light."

Dante understood that the Christian intellectual tradition is rooted in concreteness. Christian thinking does not begin with general religious ideas or universal principles, but with a particular history that began in a tiny part of the world called Judea and extends across the generations and centuries in a stately procession of those who look to that light that "once seen, alone and always kindles love." For the mystery that lies at the center of Christian faith is mediated by the men and women whose lives have been illumined by that light. The Christian intellectual, then, knows that he does not traffic in ideas alone, for he perceives, with Dante, that God's ways are "buried from the eyes of everyone whose intellect has not matured within the flame of love."[16]

16. Dante quotations come from *Paradiso* 5.8 and 7.59-60, in *The Divine Comedy of Dante Alighieri*, trans. Allen Mandelbaum (Berkeley, 1982), 38, 58.